If you don't know Okongo Samson, you might find his phenomenal stories hard to believe. But if you had traveled with him to Africa as I have and seen firsthand the countless changed lives and transformed communities, you would be a believer.

His unrelenting passion to go to the darkest places with the light of the gospel led him to unspeakable suffering. With humble courage, Okongo followed God's call, and it led him to horrific abuse at the hands of brutal men. In *Abducted But Not Forsaken*, Okongo takes you on his own personal and painful journey into danger and death with great fear and even greater faith. To walk into the valley of death and escape within an inch of your life is one thing. To choose to go back to those same places of terror and torture to show love and forgiveness to those who brutalized you is quite another. It is Okongo's surprising response to that despicable brutality that sets apart this must-read book!

There is a message here for all of us. Forgiveness is one of the most powerful and liberating human experiences. Okongo took seriously the principles of forgiveness found in the Bible, and it transformed his life. Now, Okongo's life work is all about this kind of transformation. Reading this book challenges us to address the unresolved conflicts in our own life in a way that can bring true freedom to our soul.

Dr. John W. Miller
Author, pastor, and pastoral consultant,
Centers of Church Based Training, Tucson, Arizona

Even when he stayed in my house after he was released from prison in Saudi Arabia, I had no idea what his story was. It was later, as our friendship grew, that I realized I am a friend to a Christian apostle,

Okongo Samson. *Abducted But Not Forsaken* shows his character, courage, passion, and love for others, even those with whom he disagrees on views and beliefs. Not that I am proud of some of his bad experiences, but I am proud of how he uses the bad things he endured to help others unselfishly, regardless of race and religion. Disagreement of opinion does not stop Okongo from saying what he believes and doing what he feels led to do.

Reading this book had showed me that his path is guided by Allah. His story challenged me, and I know it will challenge you, no matter your background and belief. He is one of the few Christian preachers I have invited to the inter-faith discussion forum to share his story. I call Okongo my brother, and as a Muslim, I have learned from him that people of different beliefs and faith can discuss and differ in opinion without demeaning each other.

He is gifted as a storyteller with a lot of humor. I know his story will invite you to love others and forgive those who have wronged you.

Sheikh Nasser
Imam and Islamic scholar,
Riyadh, Saudi Arabia

All God's people have a God-given purpose for their lives, but few make it a priority, and even fewer dedicate their lives, and all that they do, to being the hands and feet of God. Okongo Samson is one of those people who took the latter path.

I have known Okongo since 2007 and traveled with him abroad for missions, and he is one of the few people I call a spiritual giant. His knowledge of and application of God's Word is astonishing. Then there's his personality which warms any room he enters. His storytelling is engaging, even captivating. When you read *Abducted But Not Forsaken*, you will see how God has used him to bring strength to others, restore hope to broken lives, and help people fall in love with God. I am honored to be working with many whose lives have been impacted by his ministry.

If you ever get a chance to meet with Okongo in person, take it. You will be blessed with a new friend for life, and one you will certainly be spending eternity with in Heaven if you are a follower of Jesus Christ.

Jim Weisert
Businessman, church elder,
and Unite 4 Africa board chairman,
Tucson, Arizona

Okongo Samson and his way of life helped me learn what love and peace really is, not the fear and hate I grew up knowing between different religions. It was through keenly watching what God did through him in our family that made me realize I desperately needed the Lord this man was serving. I was attracted and intrigued by him, having confidence and being so secure in what he believed that he did not care about the consequences.

When I was still a Muslim, I asked antagonizing questions early in Okongo's interaction with my family. Little did I know that I would become a follower of Christ as he eventually led me to a prayer of confession and then discipled me. My life was challenged and changed even more when I accompanied him and my dad, Ibrahim, on a trip to Mauritania and Yemen. I witnessed some of Okongo's most painful moments, and he remained calm, speaking truth in love through it all. Clearly, he is led by the Spirit of God.

I remember my dad telling him to write a book, and decades later, we have that book. *Abducted But Not Forsaken* has helped me understand details from Okongo's story and His call from God which have greatly impacted me. It is my honor to call Okongo my mentor, apostle, and a father to us all. I know this book will inspire you and your family. Take action on what God asks you to do to heal.

Rahman Abdul
Ibrahim's son, Casablanca, Morocco

In this passion-filled, captivating, true story of faith, my friend, Okongo Samson, transparently shares his journey, through heavy persecution and seasons of sweeping doubt, that led him to a deep resolve of unshakable faith. I have partnered with Okongo and the Unite 4 Africa ministry for over a decade, and I travel with him doing mission work around the globe. Okongo consistently points us to Jesus as the one who is worthy of all we have, even our very lives. He also reveals the depth of healing that can only come through the touch of Jesus.

Abducted But Not Forsaken is a must read for those who desire to see genuine, authentic Christianity in our day. Read this book and prepare to be inspired and challenged!

Kurt Dillinger
Founder and president, LIFE International,
Grand Rapids, Michigan

Have you been hurt and can't stop obsessing over what happened? Even though you know you should let it go, such bitterness can go on for ages. Putting the past behind you is quite a long and slow process.

But my brother, Okongo Samson, overcame it and stepped into the destiny God created for him, the ministry of Christ. He has succeeded because hurt no longer intrudes into his thoughts. I am proud of Okongo because he enriches the whole world with the best of God's goodness through his ministry. When he tells his story to others, it motivates them to bring healing and forgiveness, making him a Christ-like role model for us. It also brings an awareness to other Christians of what to expect and how to cope in difficult circumstances.

However, like Jesus Christ, and other legends of faith, some people might not agree with the stories, especially if it exposes their wrong deeds or their hard hearts. Yet Okongo has never been afraid because he learns and gains more experience and faith in difficult situations such as abduction, rejection, and imprisonment without justice.

As a family, we were afraid when he ventured into the Middle East where Christianity has low acceptance. He took missionary work into these areas amid all anti-social situations, and God saw him through.

Because I am the tenth in our family of 16 siblings, I know that Okongo is like a buffalo, but his wife, Shyla, calls him a gorilla. He pushes, and keeps pushing, until things get done. He persuades others to find their calling from God and even join him in his ministry. You, too, will be persuaded as you read *Abducted But Not Forsaken.*

John Owuor Okong'o
Humanitarian health worker, Médecins Sans Frontières,
Geneva, Switzerland

Abducted But Not Forsaken is the story of a great adventure of faith. But it's not fiction. You'll find yourself having a hard time believing all that Okongo Samson has endured and survived. You won't want to put this book down. It's a story of great courage wrapped in the reality of our human flesh and weakness. Okongo shows us what it means to be an authentic follower of Jesus, and this book is a powerful encouragement to anyone who wants to trust God and make a difference.

My recommendation is that you prayerfully prepare yourself before you start reading. God is about to take you on your own adventure of faith.

Glen Elliott
Lead pastor, Pantano Christian Church,
Tucson, Arizona

This is an extremely powerful story of a man of God with a big heart for others. Okongo Samson discipled me and my family while I was a Muslim until I became a follower of Christ. He has been a catalyst in my spiritual journey. The way he connects to build relationships and bridges between Christians and other religions is admirable. I was terrified and challenged the day he led me to a prayer of confession when I converted, recruiting me to go with him to Iran, my birth country, to disciple my fellow people. As a former Muslim, I learned biblical principles and grew as a man as Okongo discipled and mentored me. His story shows a man truly called by God to reach people all over the world regardless of their background.

I was young when we met him in the plane from Cairo to Lusaka, and I did not understand why my dad, Jamal, decided to have him stay with us. While he was in pain from prison, he was full of humor telling his stories. My brother and I did not know if we should laugh or not. We kept serious faces listening to his stories. It was weird, but that was when my heart started to seek the God he was serving. *Abducted But Not Forsaken* is a book that will challenge you to see how God works in ways we can never imagine or understand. I am a testimony of God's grace and love, and I can see how God used my dad to be a part of Okongo's story. I am honored that Okongo is my mentor and brother, and I am glad to be one of those people impacted by his ministry.

Farshid Ahmed
Businessman and Jamal Ahmed's son,
Lusaka, Zambia

If you want to be inspired by a modern-day, apostle Paul-like, true adventure story, this is the book for you! Okongo Samson's strength and courage to persevere against all kinds of evil, and to trust our Lord to see him through these difficult and often horrific situations, is a testimony to his faith in the one who holds it all in His hands.

Okongo grew up in an oral culture, speaking multiple languages, and he knows that stories are the language of the heart. I have no doubt that after reading *Abducted But Not Forsaken*, you will want to share this God-led and divinely inspired story with others. It is one that will be told repeatedly and for generations to come to the praise and glory of the one true God! I have never heard or read about so many difficulties that one follower of Christ has encountered over their lifetime, except for those that I have read about in the first century Christian church and the accounts of the first apostles.

Okongo's willingness to lay everything aside in his efforts to share his faith and tell the stories of the Bible with others, leading them to eternal salvation, is awe-inspiring. Okongo's ability and commitment to trust and obey the one true God through all of the difficulties he experienced is amazing and encouraging. Ultimately, though, it is his willingness to go back and offer forgiveness to those who persecuted him and sought his death that exemplifies what the Lord Jesus Christ is all about with unending mercy, grace, forgiveness, and love.

Okongo is part of my life, and I thank God for his role in strengthening and encouraging my walk, trust, and faith in Jesus Christ.

Kent Kiefer
CEO and executive director, Scriptures In Use,
Green Valley, Arizona

I have known Okongo Samson for a couple of decades. In our friendship, and serving together in our ministry, I have found him to be a man of integrity, faith, and vision, full of wisdom and humble. He has become a blessing to me, my family, my ministry, and our great continent of Africa at large. *Abducted But Not Forsaken* is an amazing book packed full of important biblical principles on how to respond to suffering and challenges, including his personal stories and life and ministry experiences. This book gives hope for those who have been passing through various life hardships in one way or another, and it will help us to deeply understand the sovereignty of God in any circumstances. It also shows us how God works for good in the lives of those of us who love God and are called according to His will.

I encourage and recommend that you give *Abducted But Not Forsaken* to your friends and loved ones so that they will experience the blessings of God in their lives and ministry through their sufferings and life challenges. Thank you, Okongo, for providing us this wonderful, eye-opening book. I always thank God for your life, vision, and ministry.

Pastor Samson Weldemariam
Vice president and Africa director of Unite 4 Africa, Inc.,
and vice president of Emmanuel United Church of Ethiopia, Africa

Our first meeting with Okongo Samson and his wife, Shyla, proved to be an instant heart connection. We met Shyla when we taught a School of Prayer in Tucson, Arizona, and she graciously invited us to their home to spend a little more time together. We were excited to discover that our new friendship with the Samsons was also a connection as co-laborers with Christ and partners in the gospel.

There are many similarities in our ministries. In our healing prayer ministry, we often tell people that healing is only theoretical until it is put to the test. The veracity of Okongo's healing from physical, emotional, and spiritual pain is evident as he describes his journey through imprisonment, abuse, and torture for the sake of the gospel. His practice of forgiving his abusers, as well as the ministry of reconciliation that he now leads, bear witness to the healing grace of God in his life.

It is our prayer that *Abducted But Not Forsaken* will be more than just an interesting story about the trials and triumphs of an exceptional ambassador for Christ. We believe that it will lead each reader into a deeper understanding of how the practice of forgiveness can bring total freedom from even the worst experiences of trauma.

Calvin and Julie Tadema
Authors, speakers, and founders and
directors of Master's Mind Ministry,
Bush Prairie, Washington

I grew up with Okongo Samson in the small village of Kandaria. We became very good friends after he transferred to the middle school that I was attending, and we spent most of the time together. In class, we were desk mates, on the playground we played together, and after school we walked home together. We shared meals on a daily basis.

As middle school kids, we believed in each other. I could trust Okongo, and he trusted me. Because we were very competitive, we worked hard in school and gained the trust of our teachers and fellow students. As a result, we became class leaders and mentors to our peers both in academics and school activities. Okongo was a very serious student who believed in following directions and instructions, and that made one of our teachers, Mr. Awiti, love him very much.

Mr. Awiti took the time to teach us about theology and philosophy as exemplified by great men in the Bible. He inspired us to live a moral life and taught us how Moses rescued his people from bondage. It never occurred to me that my friend Okongo would go through the same temptations and trials that many disciples and great men of God have gone through.

Abducted But Not Forsaken provides an in-depth account of Okongo's life story and the experiences that shaped his ethics, his belief in God, and his desire to help spread the Word of God to non-believers. He shares remarkable stories about growing up in Kenya, and his imprisonments, abuse, and torture. Growing up with Okongo, I always knew that he was a courageous person who believed in accomplishing his goals. I never imagined that he would suffer the way he has explained in this book. Yet I believe that his childhood life prepared him to endure those sufferings. He never saw his childhood hardships as obstacles, but challenges to overcome.

One thing that I admired in Okongo, and still do, is that he has always been a person of faith and courage. Okongo is a great man who has touched many lives, and his amazing revelations in this book will surely engage the thoughts of readers for a long time.

Dr. Anthony Ananga
Assistant professor and department chair,
Florida A&M University, Tallahassee, Florida

Forgiveness. It is a life maker or life breaker, and other than the story of Jesus, I know of few life stories of the true application of forgiveness in the life of a modern-day disciple than that of Okongo Samson. How can you go back to over a dozen prisons where you were abused and tortured, ask to see the man in charge, and tell him to his face that you forgive him for what he did to you? His book tells the story of how all this happened and the results of Okongo's demonstrated Christlike forgiveness to them. It's a truly amazing story of God's work, first in the life of Okongo and how it spread to others.

Now, really, this is a must read.

John Hendee
Author and team expansion evangelism trainer
and chair of World Evangelism at Hope International University,
San Diego, California

I first met Okongo and his wonderful wife, Shyla, a few years ago, and it did not take long for me to realize that he was a special messenger for the Gospel of Jesus Christ our Savior. This wonderful book includes some of the details of what happened and of the lives God touched, beginning with his own, as an obedient servant of Jesus. I was stunned and overwhelmed by the sacrifices Okongo was willing to make in order to reach those who do not want to hear the life-saving story of God's Son! This book's principles of commitment will not only change your life but will impact those around you!

Charlie Bowles
Owner, Bowles Realty and Investments LLC,
Tucson, Arizona

ABDUCTED
BUT NOT FORSAKEN

How one man's escape from a
notorious terrorist brought hope to Africa

OKONGO SAMSON

Abducted But Not Forsaken
by Okongo Samson
© 2021 by Okongo Samson. All rights reserved.

Editing by Adam Colwell's WriteWorks, LLC, Adam Colwell and Ginger Colwell
Cover design by Jimmy Anaya
Interior design and typeset by Katherine Lloyd, The DESK

Published by Adam Colwell's WriteWorks, LLC

Printed in the United States of America

ISBN (Paperback): 978-1-7356969-8-0
ISBN (eBook): 978-1-7356969-9-7

CONTENTS

DONOR RECOGNITION

I'm honored to have friends who shared my vision of the work God is now doing through this book and who chose to help underwrite some of the costs of getting *Abducted But Not Forsaken* into the hands of as many people around the world as possible. I want to thank each of you for your generous gifts.

Mark Albertin

Norma Hunt Allen

Rev. Al Aponte

Genevieve Aquino

Richard and Kathleen Atkinson

Dave Beeson

Michael Birrer

Bryan and Sandy Brock

Patricia Brophy

Chad and Kendall Brown

David and Karyn Buser

Tasha Campbell

Scott Carmon

James and Susan Covello

Kent and Anita Chambers

Paul and Nancy De Young

Darian and Lea Domes

Adam and Jessica Dunaway

Thomas and Jeanne Dwan

Glen and Jolene Elliott

Bill and Kim Folven

Laverne Foster

James and Mary Gaynor

Ben and Kelly Genzman

Ryan and Dannaka Genzman

Rory and Lesia George

Matthew and Jeanette Griebel

Kathy Hammond

Marc and Joanie Hammond

Norman and Barb Hawkins

Terry and Monica Hendricks

Phil and Janet Hobbs

Maurice and Ruth Holthaus

Larry Horton

Debbie Kazal

Diane Kephart

Andrea King

Kraig and Stacey Kishbaugh

Randy and Nancy Klug
David and Robin Knoble
James and Linda Kress
Living Way Ministry
Gary Loveley
Greg and Beth Lynch
Robert Mangene
Brent and Lisa Martin
Jeff and Allison Martin
Steve Miller
Jimmy and Liz Morales
Paul and Donna Mueller
Martin and Cynthia Neuens
Mark and Kim Newhouse
Jenifer Nichols
Joyce Nott
Don and Jeannette Oliver
Thomas and Tina Papale
Amy Pederson
Jerry and Janet Pipes
Lance and Sue Pope
Tom and Julie Porfirio

Fred Porter
Mark and Leanne Ragel
Jeff and Shelley Reich
Randy and June Reynolds
Rod and Jeannie Robison
Joseph and Lisa Sathre
Larry and Dianne Schultz
Greg and Valerie Semlow
Paul Siegel
Brad Smith
Cody and JoAnne Stephens
Bill and Tammi Stevens
Jeff and Chris Stewart
Bill and Jan Thigpen
Ilene Thompson
Robert and Lori Tucker
John and Dani Utz
Melanie Vaughn
Joe and Mary Wambach
Jim and Beth Weisert
Nathan Wilson

ACKNOWLEDGEMENTS

First and foremost, I want to express my gratitude to my Heavenly Father and Jesus Christ my Lord and Savior. There is absolutely nothing impossible with God. Thank you, God, for your calling on my life. You are my guide, counselor, comforter, deliverer, and healer as I serve you. Even though there were times when I was hopeless and wanted to quit, you did not abandon me or forsake me. You provided the strength and courage for this work. The stories in this book are your stories—and to you I give all the glory, honor, and praise!

To my beloved, gentle, and loving wife, Shyla, who has stood with me ever since I met her. You are the best and most wonderfully supportive friend I know. God blessed me far beyond what I had imagined with you. I acknowledge my late mother, Judith, who poured wisdom into my life, and my dad, Jeck, who is a pillar to this date. Many thanks to the late Maria, who gave me hope when I escaped from my captors in northern Uganda.

To each of our family members, friends, and co-laborers in the ministry who have supported us and prayed for us season after season, thank you! To the many leaders and believers God has put in my life who left their families, homes, jobs, comfort, and safety to travel with me to different parts of the world to share the good news, thank you! To the Unite 4 Africa board of directors serving with God's guidance to make the vision of the ministry come to pass, thank you! Your blessings and rewards await in Heaven!

To our intercessors and financial partners, I cannot thank you enough for standing in the gap and for your diligence in your prayers for us to be obedient to God's will, especially during challenging times! God greatly uses you to empower me to empower others spiritually, emotionally, spiritually, and economically, bringing abundant life in Christ. May God reward you!

I acknowledge my fellow co-workers who were persecuted and some, as a result, who became martyrs. I still remember the words you spoke the moment you were transitioning into Heaven while I remained here to serve God. I thank God for your lives! To the many new believers from other faiths who took the risks of persecution and gave up everything to follow Jesus, it is not easy to give up your homes, job, possessions, and lives as you humbly follow Jesus Christ our Lord. Thank you!

I would like to thank all who helped me with their input for this book, especially those who worked diligently in the editing process. Adam and Ginger Colwell, your deep faith, gifts, and support cannot be repaid. Some days I didn't really want to write, but you encouraged and ministered to me in the process and had great belief in me. Thank you! To my friend, Rod Robison, who recognized my story was one worth sharing with the world and put the plans together at a lunch meeting where you said, "This is it, Okongo. You gotta do it, and your stories will offer hope." Now we have the book. God bless you, Rod and Jeannie, for your inspiration.

I want to thank Glen Elliott, John Miller, Randy Reynolds, Calvin and Julie Tadema, and Charlie Bowles, among others. You have prayed with me and offered wisdom step by step. God bless you!

Finally, writing this book has pulled things out of my memory that I could not have had the opportunity to share in one sitting or during my short speaking events. I now realize that sharing my experiences honestly and vulnerably will not only help many others tell their story, but it will lead them to seek forgiveness from those who have hurt them and the ones they have hurt, bringing healing. Glory to God!

FOREWORD

Randy Reynolds

Founder and Executive Director of Community Renewal
Tucson, Arizona

What a story! Okongo Samson is truly a man of great faith and courage who has had amazing experiences that have touched and inspired me, as well as many others. The level of violent abuse that has come his way makes me feel like I don't really take any risks for Christ's Kingdom, even though I know we all have different calls from the Caller. In Africa and the Middle East, the violence is physical. In America, it is verbal.

In the Kingdom of God, reconciliation is a primary mission given by our King, and Okongo has chosen to embrace that purpose in his life. I admire the deep devotion that causes Okongo to seek God through His Word, find healing, and grant his abusers forgiveness. He communicates his humanity like the psalmist and also demonstrates the devotion to God that sparks the divine within him. Very few books have stories as engaging as this one, and I am so glad you will get the chance to hear him tell his story as you read.

The drama of this story is massive enough for the big screen, and I hope it is translated into a movie. Just like in the motion picture *Hacksaw Ridge,* Okongo should get a medal of honor for his "conspicuous gallantry and intrepidity involving risk of life above and beyond the call of duty." Heroes of the faith inspire us to faith, to patience, and to embrace the promises of God to receive the strength to carry out the tasks He gives us. This is obvious in Okongo's brokenness and in how he finds healing and courage in his relationship with Christ.

Today, we live in a polarized world. Part of the world takes freedom to the extreme and punishes those who may set limits on individual freedom. The other half is autocratic and authoritarian and will punish those who are not conforming to the rigidity of their system. Okongo has the courage to stand up for grace and truth. Even if it brings punitive consequences his way, he is willing to accept them. The body of Christ needs more people who can stand up for God's truth yet grant grace to those who are offensive. This book will challenge you to understand the call of Christ and to manifest grace and truth in contexts that are very uncomfortable.

God brings people in difficult times to inspire us, in the light of present trials, and to help us face our own hardships with strength and courage. In 1 Chronicles 28:20, David tells his son Solomon, "Be strong and courageous, and do the work. Do not be afraid or discouraged, for the Lord God, my God, is with you. He will not fail you or forsake you until all the work for the service of the temple of the Lord is finished."

Okongo Samson has embraced this God who has suffered for us, served us, and now leads His people in call and mission. This firsthand account and amazing drama of Okongo's tenacious faith and commitment to reconcile with his captors will stimulate your faith and inspire you to trust God to fulfill His call and mission in your life.

NOTE FROM THE AUTHOR

The events depicted in this book are related as best I remember them. Others may have a different recollection. I did my best not to misrepresent anyone in any way. I chose, in some cases, not to use individual's actual names so as to protect their privacy. Likewise, I intentionally kept specific timeframes vague.

This represents my story as a believer in Christ. Your story is different than mine, but it is just as important. You do not have to experience what I did to be a strong person of faith. Simply obey God's calling in your life, and He will use you mightily and for His glory.

Psalm 115:1
Not to us, Lord, not to us
but to your name be the glory,
because of your love and faithfulness.

PREFACE

Pastor Jack Obong'o Okong'o

*Christian counselor with doctorates in practical theology
and counseling psychology
Nairobi, Kenya*

Christians often greatly enjoy talking about the provision of God and of how Christ defeated sin on the cross and gave us the Holy Spirit to empower us to victory over sin—and rightfully so. But many times, we do not as readily talk about our own responsibility to walk in holiness, take courage in enduring torture and hostile treatment for the sake of the gospel, and then go ahead to share our experience with others.

This is a book of its own time in history. *Abducted But Not Forsaken* describes the life and experiences of my brother, Okongo Samson, a minister of the Word and a servant of God called to weather all kinds of odds to take the gospel to countries known for their blatant hostile attitude toward the gospel. The purpose of this book is to be a testimony of the power and grace of God shown in the life of one of those He has called to extraordinary ministry. It is intended to strengthen the faith not only of the author, but also those who already believe. It is aimed at motivating the people of God to understand that the Kingdom of God is not built from a comfort zone.

This book is also a true testimony of how God can call and use His own to reach religiously and culturally strange places in the world with the gospel. This is a story of the fact that fishermen must always go to where the fish are located to be successful in difficult countries. Okongo is the fifteenth born of a humble family of 16 children, and I am proud to be his elder brother. As a young man in his very early years, Okongo became passionate about God, and it was evident enough that God's call to ministry compelled him to take the gospel to the unreached people of the world. The command of Christ, "Go Ye and Make disciples of all Nations," proved urgent, in that Okongo was already reaching out to churches and schools within, and outside of the vicinity of, his childhood home in Kenya. Okongo grew up as a lighthearted man, humorous and excited about life and work. He found it easy and exciting to work on our father's farm and take the cattle out to the field to graze. I followed his development and his walk with God with much legitimate pride springing from gratitude to God for the fruitful giftedness and choice I felt, and still feel, as a chosen servant and minister of the gospel.

In his prayerful and God-driven decision, Okongo resolved to be like Paul, all things to all men so that he might by all means save some (1 Corinthians 9:22). By this willing spirit, God affirmed his call, and Okongo took a step of faith to travel to the far lands to preach the gospel. However, when I learned of the countries he had gone to, those hard-core countries who do not readily welcome the Word, I was scared for him, as were the rest of our family members. My big question was, "How could this young and vulnerable man risk his life to travel to these countries where the possibility of being killed is very high?"

It was obvious that Okongo had a clear conscience and conviction to cross over to the harvest land with a strong Christian belief that God's call was His call. He heeded God's call and obeyed Him to take the gospel to countries dominated by Hindu and Muslim faiths. For us as a family, it was hard to reach him and even hear from him. Fear gripped us as a family. My thought was that my brother was no more. The emotional pain became more intense when Okongo showed up and gave us His narrative of how he had been beaten, tortured, and imprisoned for the sake of the gospel.

However, I quickly remembered the words of the Apostle Paul. "We put no stumbling block in anyone's path, so that our ministry will not be discredited. Rather, as servants of God we commend ourselves in every way: in great endurance; in troubles, hardships and distresses; in beatings, imprisonments and riots; in hard work, sleepless nights and hunger; in purity, understanding, patience and kindness; in the Holy Spirit and in sincere love; in truthful speech and in the power of God; with weapons of righteousness in the right hand and in the left; through glory and dishonor, bad report and good report; genuine, yet regarded as impostors; known, yet regarded as unknown; dying, and yet we live on; beaten, and yet not killed; sorrowful, yet always rejoicing; poor, yet making many rich; having nothing, and yet possessing everything." (2 Corinthians 6:3-10)

Abducted But Not Forsaken powerfully depicts how a minister of God—called by God, filled with the power of the Holy Spirit, and buoyed by the love of Jesus—can go beyond his country into spheres where the gospel is not popular and where the residents can be hostile to the gospel-bearer. I have full confidence in the Lord that Okongo fulfilled the scriptural call, in obedience to Acts 1:8, which says, "But you will receive power when the Holy Spirit comes on you; and you will be my witnesses in Jerusalem, and in all Judea and Samaria, and to the ends of the earth." Certain of his call, filled with the Spirit's power, and compelled by the love of God and God's people, Okongo had no choice but to go forth in faith and courage to face the harsh treatment, taking the risk of harm and death to bring the salvation message of hope to a lost world.

This noble book, born out of indescribable travail, has a message that is needed by those who desire to live for God and serve

Him in whatever way it takes. It is a powerful testimony of how a successful ministry in difficult situations can be a powerful tool of bringing peace, hope, and reconciliation when the gospel finally brings spiritual change in the lives of the redeemed, be they hostile, murderers, or enemies of the gospel. Our Lord Jesus Christ, by His grace, is the ultimate redeemer of lost people in all nations and the only one who rebuilds a life broken by torture and beatings for the glory of His name.

Paul correctly said, "For what we preach is not ourselves, but Jesus Christ as Lord, and ourselves as your servants for Jesus' sake. For God, who said, 'Let light shine out of darkness,' made his light shine in our hearts to give us the light of the knowledge of God's glory displayed in the face of Christ. But we have this treasure in jars of clay to show that this all-surpassing power is from God and not from us. We are hard pressed on every side, but not crushed; perplexed, but not in despair; persecuted, but not abandoned; struck down, but not destroyed." (2 Corinthians 4:5-9) This is the joy and celebration of the author and his message to the Christian church for the building of the Kingdom of God.

To read this book is to enjoy and reflect on the clear, beautifully organized thoughts of a man of God who became justly famous in this generation as one who experienced pain and torture, but whom God used to bring forgiveness, healing, reconciliation, peace, and more. I trust this book will inspire and strengthen the faith of all readers to know that to whom God sends, He promises, "Surely I am with you always, to the very end of the age." (Matthew 28:20)

ABDUCTED
BUT NOT FORSAKEN

Chapter 1

ABDUCTION AND ESCAPE

I *want to go.*
The words compelled me then just as they do today.

I want to go.

The possible perils of where I was going didn't matter, not when compared to the calling burning in my heart.

People don't want to go because of those perils? I thought. *This is my opportunity. I'll go. I know how to run. If they want to capture me, I will run into the bush.*

I was naïve, yes, but I was also bold. Most 16-year-olds are, and where I come from in Kenya, I had been taught to be bold since the day I was born. So, on that particular sunny afternoon, riding in the chartered matatu minibus heading away from my childhood village and into northern Uganda for the first time, I wasn't afraid.

Instead, I was excited.

Thrilled.

I couldn't wait to get there.

I was travelling with a German missions group called DIGUNA (*Dei gute Nachricht für fur Afrika*, meaning, "The good news for Africa") that went to communities throughout east and central Africa to show the Jesus Film and tell the villagers how they could give their lives to Christ and find salvation in Him. There's singing

1

and speaking, just like a little church service. The group had come to my village one year earlier, just after I had been saved. Since then, I had accompanied the group and told the story of how I came to know Christ in other communities in Kenya.

So, when I learned DIGUNA was going into northern Uganda but no one wanted to go because it was too dangerous, I, on the other hand, couldn't resist.

It wasn't going to be an easy trip. We expected the journey to take three days because of the road conditions and stops along the way, and the big, retrofitted German army truck carrying all of the equipment had departed several hours before we did in the matatu. There were about 40 of us crammed into the minibus, but only myself and two others were heading to the mission site. The rest of the passengers were going to different destinations.

As I sat in the middle seat near the front of the bus, I thought back, as I had many times before, to that wonderful moment when I first met the living God. My parents, Jeck and Judith, had become believers in Jesus before I was born through missionaries who came to Kenya from England in the mid-1900s when Kenya was still a British colony. As the second youngest of their 16 children, I saw that what my parents had experienced was real, and I wanted it for myself.

I'd given my heart to Christ at a Christian youth camp that I wasn't even supposed to attend. The only reason I was there was that my father had told me to walk with one of the camp's speakers and carry his luggage from my village near Lake Victoria to the camp. It was a five-hour trek through rugged terrain, and I was barefoot because I had never owned a pair of shoes. By the time we arrived, I had so many thorns in my legs that I decided I'd stay there for the night, avoid the risk of harm from wild animals, remove the thorns, and return home the next day.

Until then, I thought Christianity was only for those who had closely interacted with a white missionary. I had previously heard these missionaries declare the message of Christ through an interpreter, but their presentation was dull and boring. What I did like about them was their big vehicles, the large houses they built in the settlements where they stayed, and the gifts they gave out to villagers: books, snacks, and especially honey. I loved honey like a Pooh bear.

However, the person my father asked me to take to the youth camp wasn't white. In fact, when I got there, I saw that no one at the camp was white. So, when I heard African men passionately preaching Christ, it was amazing. They gave an emotional altar call, asking people to come up to accept Jesus as Savior, complete with the singing of hymns such as "Pass Me Not, O Gentle Savior" and "I Give Myself Away." The preaching was exciting, and the music tugged at my heart. It went on and on until midnight.

I responded to the altar call that night and ended up staying there for three more days until the youth camp ended. I was 15.

One week after I was saved, I was at home laying on a *parr*, a grass fiber mat that served as my bed. Everyone slept together near one another. By the light of a kerosene lamp, I had just finished reading a passage from the Bible I had received as a gift at the camp. It was from the book of John, which I had been reading daily along with the Psalms ever since I accepted Jesus. I was still easily brought to tears since my decision, and I was crying once more as I thought about what I had just read from the Bible.

Then I heard it.

Heard *Him.*

God's voice—physically audible and as clear as if He were sitting right there in the room next to me. No one else laying nearby heard it, only me.

He said, "I want to use you to the uttermost parts of the world to bring transformation to many people who are in need spiritually, socially, emotionally, physically, and economically, and to bring healing. You will go through challenges."

His call was quite specific, and it was accompanied by a vision of me with crowds of people in different countries around the world. In some of those images, I was leading the crowds.

But it really didn't make sense to me. I never thought then that I would someday lead diverse groups of people around the world the way I am today. At that point, I thought leaders had to come from either foreign countries or local wealthy families. In addition, I grew up in a place where my family struggled to have the basics of food and clothing. I had never travelled to any significant town or city outside of my remote village.

Spiritually, I connected to what God was saying, and I quietly responded, "I am ready, Lord, for the challenges. Bring it on!"

Later, I'd sometimes wish He hadn't said that I'd go through challenges. I had no idea how severe they would become. I also knew I had felt a void without God and wanted to tell others about Him. But to meet the physical needs of others to the "uttermost parts," or even to serve these people when my own needs were so great? It was hard for me to reconcile the two.

> **"I am ready, Lord, for the challenges. Bring it on!"**

"How can this be?" I wondered aloud. "I don't know what the uttermost parts of the world are. How will I reach there?"

It sounded like a vain dream or imagination, but God's voice kept saying, "I want to use you to the uttermost parts of the world."

As the matatu pounded down the road, I reflected on that calling and marveled at how it had started coming to pass, even if in just a small way, in the one year since that night. I had shared my salvation story many times in village settings such as homes and schools, or in gatherings like weddings or funerals, throughout the region where I grew up. It was through this kind of simple storytelling that the gospel message spread, and I was amazed as people responded to it by choosing to give their lives to Jesus.

I was filled with an undeniable joy as I looked ahead, out through the windshield, and thought about what wonderful things might happen when we reached northern Uganda. We'd speak to the people, for the very first time, about Christ and His love for them, and perhaps even rescue the children I'd heard were in danger there by bringing God's truth to people involved with the radical groups who kidnapped and abused them.

I bowed my head and closed my eyes, both in silent, thankful prayer and in sleepy tiredness from the long, bumpy ride, as I thought about all God had done.

Therefore, I had no warning when, suddenly, the minibus screeched to a halt, the brakes squealing as dust flew off the road and temporarily obscured my view.

As the brown cloud dispersed, I first noticed the massive log that had been laid in front of the matatu to force it to come to a stop.

Then I saw the men—about a dozen of them, dressed in khaki, some wearing torn rags, and all holding automatic weapons.

As I struggled to fully wake up, I had no idea whether or not we were already in northern Uganda, nor did I know who these men were: troops from the government of Uganda or rebels who went into villages to terrorize people and abduct children. But I did know they didn't have a uniform like the regular army I had always recognized in Kenya.

It was that unknown that scared me more than anything else. They could be good soldiers. They could be bad ones. There was no way to tell. I did recall that one of the bad groups, the Lord's Resistance Army, had always kidnapped people by going into the villages themselves, not from hijacking vehicles on the road. I didn't think it could be them.

Whoever it was surrounded the minibus and ordered everyone to get out. We were then ordered to remove everything from our pockets, put it on the ground, and lay chest down onto the dirt. They took all of our possessions, including our bags and any identification we had amongst our belongings. They also gathered up everything we had dropped onto the ground.

I couldn't see any of this because we weren't allowed to raise our heads, but I knew what was happening. Chin down, I lifted up my eyes just enough to quickly spy the area around me. The soldiers were everywhere. I didn't even think about running.

Whoever they were, and whatever they intended, I knew we were in trouble.

I took a deep breath. My heart pounded. All I could do was hope for the best.

Next thing I knew, we were all told to get back inside. One of the soldiers took the wheel. A few more got into the matatu with us. I had never been that close to an armed soldier, and it frightened me. Stories my father had told me about his knowledge of the military invaded my thoughts—that if soldiers took you, you were as good as dead.

Remembering those stories only amplified my fear.

As the minibus sputtered back to life, I closed my eyes once more, but it wasn't from excitement or weariness.

I was afraid—and I prayed.

God, please let them drive us to a safer place.

We drove for only a mile, no more than that, and then veered sharply to the right, onto another road heading into the forest. From where I was now seated in the back of the vehicle, I saw tropical, dense trees with a thick overhanging canopy that was like nothing I had ever seen before. The scenery was incredibly beautiful, but I was so filled with fear I couldn't enjoy it. As we journeyed further into the forest and away from the main road, I started to wonder if I had made the right choice to go to northern Uganda. I heard the voices of my father and some of my older siblings telling me to wait. I recalled my mother telling me not to go, even though she said she was proud of why I wanted to do so.

But God had spoken. It was an opportunity He'd created.

I had to go.

But I couldn't help but ask myself.

Have I made a mistake?

Doubt was still haunting me when the matatu came to a halt. We were ordered outside the vehicle and then told to walk forward.

As we trod ahead surrounded by the armed men, we approached a clearing and what appeared to be a camp. It was enclosed by a tall fence made of different sized logs of wood, stacked side-by-side. There were no posts between the sections. The thick, round trunks of the forest trees served as the posts. The barrier surrounded the camp. I couldn't see through it.

One of the soldiers opened the gate, and as we went in, I saw more soldiers—and hundreds of children.

Boys and girls. Little ones that could've been as young as five. Teens my age or older.

They were everywhere, and I'll never forget the look on their faces. Their blank stares betrayed the trauma they were experiencing.

Here I was, among them.

I looked around and noticed that the adults who had been in the matatu were nowhere to be seen. I had no idea where they had been taken. I saw how far away the fence was from the corner of the camp where the rest of us, all children or youngsters, had been gathered. Beyond the fence was nothing but trees and canopy so thick I couldn't tell if it was day or night. Only the kerosene lamps provided what light there was in the gloomy darkness.

Fear gripped me. I was racked to pieces.

I was trapped.

There has to be a way out.

When I hoped the soldiers weren't looking, I slowly moved toward the fence. I saw a line on the ground and carefully crossed over it.

If I can just spot one opening big enough for me to squeeze through, or a place in the fence short enough for me to leap over, maybe—

Hands suddenly reached out and cruelly yanked me away from the barrier.

I'd been seen and caught.

Nausea swept through me as I was ordered to remove my shirt, pull down my khaki shorts and underwear, and lie face down on the ground.

The switch was sharp and flexible. It slashed across my bare butt, how many times I don't remember.

Never before had I been hit with such brutal force. All I felt was stinging, total pain.

Tears filled my eyes, but I refused to cry. Crying would've only brought more lashes from the switch.

"Get up! Go over there!"

I did as I was told, and at that moment, horror overwhelmed me as I realized where I must be.

I was in the camp of the Lord's Resistance Army—the abductors and abusers of children.

There were no structures. There was just the ground, the fence, and the forest. None of the other captives glanced my way when I returned to the group. They knew what had happened to me because it had already happened to them. Numerous times, I imagined. There was nothing to say, nothing to do.

I hoped I wouldn't be punished again. I hoped they would release us.

I hoped when there was no visible reason to hope.

I had never felt anything like this. I had never seen anything like this.

I was at a loss, waiting for whatever was going to happen next.

In the distance across the camp, I saw that some of the children were being shown how to use guns. Others were marching.

They're being trained to fight, I concluded. *Perhaps the adults were already taken away to the front lines.* I needed time to make some sense of it all.

But I wasn't given time. More soldiers suddenly approached our group. They were chewing *miraa*, a plant ingested as a stimulant also known at *khat*, and smoking *bangi*, thick marijuana cigarettes.

One of them yelled in a high-pitched, angry tone, "Take off all of your clothes!"

Some of them were laughing. All of them had expressions that sickened me, a combination of aggression and lust that was pure evil.

Everyone obeyed—and then the soldiers yanked down their own pants.

They took us. Boys. Girls.

It didn't matter.

Several soldiers came to me, knocked me down, and mounted me. When I tried to fight them off, they beat me and then took me anyway.

I had just come into the camp that day. I was fresh.

It happened again and again. They took turns. I stopped fighting back.

I simply let it happen.

I had no choice.

In between, I was so sore I couldn't sit properly. I was bruised. I bled.

Surprisingly, I didn't think about my family. I didn't think about my calling from the Lord. I hardly thought about anything except my pain and the moans and cries of all those around me.

God.

What is going on here?

While I knew several tribal languages, I couldn't understand what everyone around me was saying because their languages were unknown to me. But those whose words I could recognize spoke of the trauma they had been experiencing for days. Weeks. Months. It was appalling and gruesome. I had also noticed earlier how many of them walked as though they were bowlegged, legs apart and in obvious discomfort.

I now knew why.

The days and nights that followed became a dreadful, nightmarish routine. I was coerced into learning how to march and use guns. I was raped non-stop. One after another violated me.

Surely I slept, but I don't recall ever truly doing so. Two daily meals of vegetables, leaves, and corn were made by us for the soldiers, and we ate what was left after they were fed. I was not familiar with some of the food we prepared. At times, we were given raw meat to mix in. It was rumored that some of the protein could be human flesh from those who had died in the camp or in battle.

I never found out if that was true. I ate it anyway. It was the only way I could survive.

I often wondered why I should even try to live. I'd heard from others that if I attempted to escape over the wall, I'd be shot and killed. I'd also heard that if I was sent to the front lines to fight, I'd be shot and killed there, too. Death was all around me, and I believed I was indeed slowly dying.

I was going to die. It was just a matter of when and where.

Death has a smell. It permeated my senses. It was all there was.

My existence was one of depression, anger, stress, and shame. I felt dirty and unhuman.

Before long, I couldn't handle it any longer.

I decided I was going to walk out of the camp.

Let them shoot me. That'll be the easier, less painful option.

I'd discovered the camp had two gates, one on each end. Neither was locked. After the soldiers abused us, they ate. That was the only time the camp was quiet.

That was when I walked.

I was ready to die. Before I departed, I told a fellow captive, "You might end up eating my meat."

If I'm going to die anyway, I would rather die doing something.

I chose the same gate I first came in through. The walk was painful and more of a waddle, but I straightened my back as best as I could as I strode forward. The gate was open, and while I expected a guard to be present, no one was there. I presumed he was eating.

I walked through the gate and saw the unmanned mounted gun next to the entrance. I walked past it. I fixed my eyes straight ahead.

I expected to hear the shot, feel the bullet, fall to the ground, and let the blackness take me.

I kept walking—following only the ruts of the tire tracks left by the vehicles that came in and out of the camp. I had no idea where I was. I had no sense of direction. It was the only path I could find.

I still expected to die at any moment. It was dark practically all of the time. I could barely see. A truck could come. A soldier could appear from out of the forest. Anything could happen.

I kept walking.

Then the dense brush broke, and I struggled up a small hill. As I crested it, I saw that I had arrived at a market. People walked long distances to such places to get their food and other supplies. It was morning.

I kept walking.

I entered the square where merchants sold their eggs, produce, and other farm-produced food on market day. Buildings with grass thatch roofs lined the main dirt road. People walked this way and that. They avoided me because I was naked. Anyone naked was considered to be bad or mentally ill. The villagers either looked the other way or went in the opposite direction.

Everyone except her.

She was an older woman wearing a colorful *leso* sarong dress and head wrap. She did not move away.

I approached her and vaguely told her what had happened to me. I was trembling with fatigue.

She understood my language and listened to what I had to say. She then removed her *leso* head scarf and wrapped it around my waist. It covered me down to my knees.

The woman did not smile, but I saw something in her eyes. She looked at me like I was her grandson.

It was compassion.

No, it was more than that. It was compassion and grief.

"There were some people travelling near here, and their van was captured weeks ago," she told me, tears running down her cheeks. "The military got the van, then took it to the army barracks and police station." She pointed down the road toward a distant signpost. "It's that way. It's not far. You'll see it."

With that, the kind woman offered me some corn porridge she was taking with her to the farm where she lived, and then she sent me on my way. It was a longer walk than she made it sound, about eight miles or so.

Even then, I kept walking. I still feared I could be captured again or killed on the spot.

When I finally got to the police station, I was exhausted and hungry. I was also consumed with doubt, confusion, and anger. I hurt all over. I was wrecked and overwhelmed with despair.

An officer saw me and commanded me to go inside. As I had with the woman, I explained what had happened to me as best I could. I was tirelessly interrogated by two members of the Ugandan police, and as I was, my fear increased. I was not prepared to share the savagery I had endured, yet the questioning persisted. Often, I wasn't sure how to answer some of the queries, and that kept me on edge. I was afraid my responses might somehow get me in trouble if I didn't provide the information they wanted. I didn't want them to think I was hiding anything.

Eventually, I did learn from them that the van confiscated by the military was indeed the same matatu that I was riding in when I was abducted with everyone else on board.

The officers then left the room. One of them returned moments later with my ID and my baptism card, which was an important document back then when travelling in Africa.

As I sat there, wincing while another stab of pain jarred my backside, I looked at the photo on the ID and read the words on the card—and I suddenly realized something.

It was me. I wept.

Me.

Simply seeing proof of my identity helped give me back my identity.

I had lost myself in all the horrors that were done to me at the rebel camp.

It was then, and only then, that I knew God was going to send me back home.

Only then did I think once more about my family.

Only then did I dare to consider having hope again.

I remained at the police station the rest of that day and into the next. I was provided a pair of shorts and a t-shirt to wear. My accommodations were basic: a small room with no beddings and no window, only a long bench along the wall. I slept on the mud floor because I needed the rest. I had walked all night, my legs were tired, my body was sore, and my mind was exhausted. I was ill from everything that had happened to me and was given malaria pills as a precaution. I was hungry, but I had no appetite. I was offered a big chunk of meat, but I could not eat it.

Midway through my second day there, I was told to ride along with a convoy of police heading back southeast toward Kenya, where I'd be placed on a matatu somewhere along the way. The thought of getting on another minibus terrified me. It could be hijacked like the last one I was on. But it was my only option, and I ended up riding on no less than four different matatus before my journey ended.

In all, it would take another three days, but I had made it.

Somehow, I had survived.

I was going home.

When I finally arrived at my village, I was told that I had been gone for about four weeks. Taking into account the amount of time it took me to escape, be processed at the station, and then make my way back to my village, I must've been in the camp for a couple of weeks, perhaps longer.

I don't think I'll ever remember for sure how long I was held captive and abused—but I know I was extremely fortunate to have come out alive. The Lord's Resistance Army (LRA) abducted more than 30,000 boys and girls before and after the time I was taken by them. Children were indeed put on the front lines of combat along with adults, and they were even forced to kill, mutilate, and rape family members, schoolmates, neighbors, and teachers.

Birthed in 1988 in northern Uganda, the Lord's Resistance Army formed from the remnants of the Holy Spirit Movement

Army founded by Alice Lakwena, a priestess and distant relative of Joseph Kony, the leader of the LRA. Their main goal was to establish a theocracy based on the biblical Ten Commandments. Therefore, the LRA adopted a mix of Christian and esoteric ideology which they blended with traditional myths. Their atrocities went on until the Lord's Resistance Army was largely expelled from Uganda by the end of 2006. In July 2005, the International Criminal Court issued warrants against commanders of the group, and they were indicted on 12 counts of crimes against humanity, including murder, enslavement, sexual enslavement, and rape. Another 21 counts of war crimes were added.

But that did not stop them. The LRA relocated and became a problem in nearby countries such as the Democratic Republic of the Congo. Since 2008, the U.S. State Department estimated that the Lord's Resistance Army had killed more than 2,400 people and abducted more than 3,400 others.[*]

Of course, back when I returned to my family, I had no idea about those harsh statistical realities. But I had experienced the LRA's brutality firsthand, and that was far, far worse.

The first couple of weeks I was home, other than returning to my daily chores, I kept to myself. I wasn't feeling well, and I used that as an excuse to avoid others as much as possible. No one knew what had really happened to me yet. Everyone thought I was returning from my mission trip. But it was clear that I wasn't healthy, and that prompted some to start asking questions that I did not yet want to answer. I didn't know how to tell my story to them. I didn't even know where to begin.

I spent a lot of time thinking, internalizing all that I had been

---

[*]   Sources: "Lord's Resistance Army," Encyclopedia Britannica, https://www .britannica.com/topic/Lords-Resistance-Army, and "Profile: The Lord's Resistance Army," Aljazeera, https://www.aljazeera.com/news/africa/2011 /10/2011101418364196576.html

through. *Why did they take me? How long has this been going on? Why hasn't anything been done about it?* I also relived the painful cries of the other children in the camp, all those who didn't escape and likely were going to die or were already dead. I wondered, *How can I rescue them?* Surely, there had to be a way. As I thought about it, my anger grew stronger.

I also dreamed—horrible nightmares of what they did to me. Each time, I'd wake up trembling or in tears. I was ashamed and sad. I also felt alone. Who could possibly relate to what I had been through?

I was also filled with doubt, uncertainty born from a sense of failure because I didn't make it to my mission with DIGUNA.

Yet as I heard all of these voices in my head, another continued to break in, warring with the other thoughts and creating a battle zone in my mind.

"I want to use you to the uttermost parts of the world."

I didn't necessarily want to hear Him then, but it was that voice that eventually gave me the little bit of courage I needed to begin sharing what had happened to me.

"I want to use you to the uttermost parts of the world."

It was also that voice—persistent and loving—which began to nurture and grow what was already in my heart: a desire to help others. Whether I knew how to solve their problems or not, I wanted to see how God could use me to be there for them.

I didn't know it then, but God was going to use His promise in Romans 8:28 ("And we know that in all things God works for the good of those who love him, who have been called according to his purpose."), take the horrors I had experienced (along with others still to come), and give me a consuming passion to help others that still drives me today.

Some people just sit back and listen.

I try to make things happen.

About two weeks after returning home, I went to the pastors and elders from different churches in and around the area surrounding my village. I knew of them from the community gatherings that took place on different days each week when the church leaders came to sing, preach, and pray. I took them aside and told them bits and pieces of what I had experienced in the camp. I also shared with them my feelings of failure for not being able to do the mission.

"Well, we knew God wasn't telling you to go. It was you."

That was the response I received from some of them. The others didn't know what to say to me, at least in my presence. Their judgment, or lack of response, was discouraging and hurtful. I had hoped they would listen, pray with me, and offer me comfort from God. It didn't go that way. Even worse, they then mentioned what had happened to me in their messages to the crowds. I didn't give them permission to do that, but that didn't stop them, and they told my story in an accusatory way that made it sound as though they were adding new shame on top of the shame I already felt. It left me at a loss.

I then spoke to a few of my friends and told them what I could. That didn't help, either. They laughed and teased me. It was not a surprise. Where I was raised, males were expected to be warriors. I had been taught to conquer, but I had clearly been subdued. "Why didn't you just run away?" they challenged. No matter what I said, they did not understand that I could not run. I could not fight. I was powerless.

I'm not sure if I was looking for affirmation, encouragement, or support. I just wanted to share, and part of me thought I could find relief from my hurt and shame. But all of it left me wishing I had never told anyone anything—and now that my story was out, it spread like a wind-driven brush fire. I lived in an oral culture where people naturally told stories. Something could be said in my village and be known five miles away in no time.

As that happened, I knew the time had come to tell those closest to me and with whom I was most afraid to share: my family.

Where I grew up, families gathered together every evening to talk to one another before the meal and sometimes afterward as well. When we are actually eating, we are not supposed to speak with food in our mouths, so any conversation occurs before or after the meal itself. Usually, the father leads the discussion. In these times, family members ask questions of one another and receive responses. It's how we connect.

As I had done before, I shared a little at a time with my parents and some of my siblings. I kept everything vague because I felt so much shame regarding the abuse I had suffered. I also knew I had gone against their wishes by leaving in the first place. I was careful about what I told them. I expected negativity and rejection. I was wounded, and when people who have not been wounded respond to you, it usually doesn't come across well. They don't understand the pain. I don't blame them for that, but it makes it difficult.

Over the course of several family gatherings, I told my story. My extended family members asked questions based on what other people were saying they had heard about me. I didn't necessarily welcome the way they challenged me by asking, "Why?" I didn't have an answer for all of the questions about what I went through, why God allowed it, and why I got away and others didn't. I didn't have an answer for why I was returned to my village. After a while, I had said all I could, and I stopped.

My father was vehement, and he summed up my family's feelings. "You are alive. That's it! You came back. At least you are alive!" Eventually, some were able to say, "I'm sorry you went through that," or, "You are strong. I don't know how you handled it."

I felt both judged and accepted at the same time, but in the end, their acceptance was all that mattered.

Today, I understand the power of story—and of how telling it empowers others and helps them get through to their healing. Back then, though, it was everything I could do to find the strength to share. But I did, and as my story became more known, there were others in my village or at my school who thought I needed to go through a cleansing. It's a ceremony done by a witch doctor where a person is placed under a plastic covering beneath a blanket, made hot and sweaty as though they are in a sauna, and then given a drink that allegedly drives the uncleanness away.

Because of my faith in God, though, I didn't see it as a cleansing. I saw it as witchcraft, and I wanted nothing to do with it. Neither did my family. I'd later learn that the witch doctors would also have sex with the person in order to somehow guarantee the cleansing. This still goes on today in some places. It is abominable.

God continued to speak to me about going to the uttermost parts, but as He did, I only became angrier than I already was. I was angry at God. I was angry at Scripture. I was angry at people. I was angry at my peers. I was angry at people at church because no one wanted to sit close to me. I was often told, "If you go off on another mission, the same thing will happen to you."

I was marginalized, bitter, and confused.

It wasn't until a few women in my village reached out to me that I began to experience compassion—and truly started to have hope that things would get better. These women did not share details, but they had endured physical and sexual abuse similar to mine.

Maria was instrumental. "God will use you," she told me. "You are a good boy. God will use you to help so many people."

Maria's words resonated with the voice of God. She did not tell me exactly what had happened to her because she was elderly and did not want to bring shame to herself. But she said she understood what I had gone through. She gave me a hug.

That was the beginning. *Some people have the same story as mine,* I thought.

I am not alone.

I had spent weeks in captivity. I had been back home for three months.

But finally, finally, I could begin putting my life back together. Question was, what was I going to do with it?

Chapter 2

A DIVINE CALLING

I was raised with a legacy of perseverance and faith. My mother, Judith, was not only a wonderful mother to me and my 15 siblings, but to our entire village. Both young and old came to her, spent time with her, and benefitted from her friendship and wisdom. She was tireless, working morning to evening to care for our family with her gentle and soft-spoken manner, never raising her voice. Around 4:00 every morning during farming season from November to February, my brothers and I could hear our mother singing hymns and praying as we went to harness the ox to begin plowing the fields. There was one door going into the living room where she was and another leading into where the animals were kept.

She prayed so tenderly that we wanted to listen. "I pray for my children," she'd plea. "I bless them." It brought tears to our eyes. When she noticed us, she'd open the door and say, "I will bring *uji*," which is porridge, but then she'd keep praying, often from the book of Psalms.

I never saw her quarrel with my father. In fact, our family never fought with one another. Whenever we had differences, we worked them out. We were following the example of our parents.

My father, Jeck, was a teenager when World War II began. Kenya was a British colony, so Great Britain was seeking young

African men to go to Burma (what is now Myanmar) to fight. A person had to be 18 to go to war, but most African people didn't know their actual birthdates—or, if they did, pretended not to know and misled authorities about their age so they wouldn't have to fight. I imagine my father did know how old he was, but when he was recruited, he didn't say. When age wasn't known or declared, officials strangely checked a male's pubic hair to discern if he was old enough to go into the military. My father didn't have any, so he was left behind in Kericho, a big town known for tea cultivation, to receive more training until he was older.

In the meantime, missionaries had come to that region and noted that my father was an excellent farmer. They saw potential in him and began working with him to become a teacher. He excelled—and never had to worry about being sent to Burma. The missionaries retained Jeck as an educator, and he became one of the first teachers in western Kenya's earliest schools. He taught all subjects to every age group.

By then, all but one of my brothers and sisters had been born, and my parents taught us with some of the same strict, rigid methods (we describe it as "legalistic" today in the States) they learned from the missionaries who took in my father all those years earlier. We had to wake up at a certain time, go to school without fail unless we were truly ill, and attend church without exception, acting proper when we were there. On Sundays, we couldn't lift a tool; we could take the cows to pasture, but that was it. Everything was a command, not a suggestion. There were no excuses. I had a typical childhood for the son of a farmer and a teacher. I went into the fields around 4:00 a.m. to guide the ox all morning as it plowed, and then I looked after the other animals, including chickens and cows. None of the animals were contained. It was all open range, and we'd herd and graze the animals throughout the day before returning them to the farm each evening.

I also went hunting from a very early age. Back then, boys as young as six could go hunting, and we did not need a hunting license. We hunted to get food, but it was also to have fun. It was one of the main times, other than farming and chores, when boys and men did something together. Especially enjoyable was the fact that when we were out on the hunt, we could cuss and swear and not get in trouble like we would at home or in school. It was all a rite of passage to learn how to become a man. I still cherish those moments.

My upbringing was ideal—but my abduction by the LRA changed everything, at least during that difficult time of my life. I was very angry, and education became a way to channel my anger in a positive way. My father was preparing me to be a farmer and wanted me to go to school for that, but being a farmer wasn't me, so I took other classes without his knowledge. I was determined to learn English and other languages well and discover everything I could about other cultures. Despite my misgivings about church, I was interested in becoming a pastor.

More than anything, though, I wanted to be a doctor. I thought I needed emotional and physical healing, and I was convinced being a witch doctor wasn't the only way to heal people. I became passionate about anything medical.

My revenge for what I'd been through, and my rebellion against what others thought I should do, was to study hard. In my culture, I had the freedom to choose my own path as I got older, and that's exactly what I did. In doing so, I also rebelled against the legalistic structure that the missionaries had instilled in my father.

At times, I didn't socialize well with others at school. I was often called a geek and sometimes *Otudo*, the name of a mentally unstable man in a well-known book of African short stories that we studied in literature class. After what I had experienced, it made sense that some saw me as being odd like *Otudo*. I just didn't feel like the things they said or wanted to do were that important in comparison to the vision God's Spirit was forming in my heart. Since everyone there knew what had happened to me, though, I did take the opportunity to talk more about God. I spoke of His deliverance and freedom, and of how we can have eternal life and not die because of sin.

I was still angry at God and even disillusioned in my faith, but I proclaimed His love.

It also became a passion that drove me.

Interestingly, Christians were the skeptical ones. Many of them thought I was not good enough, was defiled, or that the Lord never called me in the first place. The vast majority of the people who paid attention to me and my story were not believers in God, and they didn't care about any of those things. All that mattered to them was that I loved them and talked about God's love for them. That drove me even more. I discovered that many of them had been wounded and had similar stories to mine, but they had no one with whom to share them. As a result of me declaring my story, they came out. I began to see that God could heal them, and I told them, "It is not what you already have. It is what you can do with what you do have."

> I was still angry at God, but I proclaimed His love.

My anger and disillusionment became my rebellion, but I saw it as rebelliousness with a cause—to reject bad things, share my story, help others experience God's love, and in the process find myself and make my own way.

Then came the time, around six months after my abduction, when I spoke for about one hour to a huge crowd of nearly 3,000 people at an open-air crusade conducted by a coalition supported by DIGUNA. It took place near Kisumu, a port city on Lake Victoria and the original capital of western Kenya. They asked me to speak, and I told the story of how I was taken captive by the

Lord's Resistance Army, why I felt God had saved me, and about God's purpose for them. I explained that when I first surrendered my life to Jesus, I was redeemed spiritually from sin. Then, when I was abducted, God helped me escape and redeemed me physically from certain death. I talked about how He did that for a purpose so that I could declare Him, even while He was teaching me how to forgive my captors for their abuse and forgive myself for my doubt.

It was there, near Kisumu, where God moved in such a way that I began to understand what God was saying when He said He wanted to use me to reach the "uttermost" parts. I saw it as the fulfillment of the vision God had given me after I was first saved. It started to solidify His calling in my life and showed me He was using my experience in Uganda to attract people to come, listen, and hear about Him. In my oral culture, people gathered in massive numbers to hear my story, a story that left them fearfully wondering how and why I had gone into such a dangerous place as Uganda and survived.

I was still afraid of rejection from others, particularly Christian leaders who were jealous of the crowds I was attracting or who didn't think I was qualified to preach. I didn't like that. I didn't feel I had to be qualified by a man when I had been qualified by God.

I was still wounded. I was still confused. I still had all that resentment and anger churning within me. But I was passionate about sharing the love of Christ, and I was seeing God working in my brokenness.

I was just like the woman by the well in John 4 who went, told people what Jesus had done for her, and many believed because of her story.

That was me.

From then on, God continued revealing Himself to me despite where I was mentally, emotionally, and spiritually. He began showing me more of who He was and what He had in store for me. I read the Bible over and over, inside and out. I wanted to know, *needed* to know, everything I could about God and His love. I didn't rely on anyone's interpretation of what the Bible said. Rather, I read it for what it was and sought to understand it. I'd read a passage five different times, and every time have a different, new revelation given to me by the Holy Spirit about that passage.

Part of what compelled me to read was the confusion I'd experienced when godly people, apparently serving the same Lord, told me different things. Some were receptive of me and my story; others were critical. As I read God's Word, I discovered that when Jesus called His disciples, He never said, "Hey, you are a fisherman, but now you have to be a theologian." Instead, Jesus simply started working with them personally, teaching them from His stories and His example. I loved that.

In the meantime, thousands were now going anywhere I spoke, and that created opportunities for me to speak in just about any setting where there was a crusade or some other large gathering. First, I went to other communities in Kenya. Before long, I was going to places across east Africa such as Sudan, Ethiopia, and Tanzania. The story of the young man who received Christ, left for a mission trip, was abducted, escaped, and was now sharing about Jesus literally went ahead of me. It spread like wildfire.

Into my late teen years onward, I spoke somewhere every weekend and went to school during the week. Schools then had assemblies every morning and sometimes in the evening, and the sharing of God's Word and prayer were a part of the assembly meetings. I spoke at a lot of those events. Public education in Kenya was based on a system of eight years of primary education followed by four years of secondary school and four years at a college or university. When I began high school, I remained passionate for knowledge. I studied everything from linguistics and religious studies to business, agriculture, history, geography, mathematics, physics, chemistry, and biology. We also had early devotions from 4:45-5:45 a.m. and again at 9:30 p.m. after evening prep studies were completed. I continued speaking in the schools, sometimes two or three in any given weekend, all while maintaining my studies.

As a speaker, I didn't need to build my own organizational structure. I'd simply be invited, and I went. When I traveled to the other places to speak, I was usually hosted by a family in the area. Africa is communal, and it was a joy for them to take me into their home. Even today with Unite 4 Africa, I enjoy staying in people's homes, even when my wife, Shyla, is with me. People will tell me, "Go to a hotel. You are a big man, a VIP!" No. I still love staying with people in their homes. It's my joy!

The first high school I attended was mixed, with both boy and girl students, and it was there where I saw bullying—and I didn't take it lightly. Once, I saw a young man grab a girl inappropriately. I immediately confronted him, and he called me a *mono*. It was a derogatory word that meant I was a "starter," a "freshman." The bottom of the totem pole.

I didn't care. Two other boys started pushing back against me, and—well, let's just say they fell on the wrong side of me physically. I grew up knowing that warriors fight for the good and defend justice no matter who they face and even if the fight gets ugly. This one did. I fought back, and I got sent home for three days. I returned, though, and remained at that school a bit longer before transferring to an all-boys school because I couldn't handle what I was seeing. Bullying did, and always will, cause my anger to take over.

During those four years of secondary education, the Lord opened up the doors for me to speak throughout east Africa. Every high school had Scripture Union, which organized large outreaches where hundreds attended. That provided opportunities for me to use those networks to form connections in communities, since I intentionally did not want to represent a particular organization or church denomination. But as my story became more well known, I started to be detained in some of the countries where I spoke. I was accused of mobilizing the community in a way that was seen as being a threat by certain groups, including some Christian organizations. On other occasions, I spoke openly against some of the leaders in the community or local government whose behavior was purely evil, from adultery and corruption to even murder. I was charged with inciting people against authority or breaking the law in some other way, and it was enough to get me incarcerated. Once after a big prayer meeting, everyone was so loud and excited, I was even charged with using and distributing drugs. It was like the Day of Pentecost in Acts 2 when it was believed the people were drunk when they were really praying in the Holy Spirit. Some communities across Africa are exuberantly passionate about their faith regardless of denomination.

I believed the only way to free people was by speaking and openly rebuking the bad things that were going on. I stood against what I believed was not right. I had already felt the pain, the torture, that bad leaders could bring, and I was willing to accept the consequences for speaking out. I was detained no less than nine times during my high school years, and each time was different. The first was in Sudan, where I was given a minimum two-month sentence and 39 lashes from a whip. However, if I could take the lashes sooner, I'd be released quicker. For example, I could request a few lashes a day for one month. That's what I did in Sudan, and I was let go early.

In each detention, I received lashes and the lengths of my stay varied. Lashes were never given in Muslim areas on holy days of prayer. In a few cases, my prison term was lessened because I

28

prayed loudly in the Holy Spirit in different languages, much like the Apostle Paul did when he was incarcerated. I was considered radical and told to get out. It was more of a potential problem to keep me than to let me go. Other times, I was released early with no explanation, though I know I was sick on some of those occasions from the appalling conditions of the prisons themselves or from the way I was treated in their custody. They likely feared I would die unless they set me free. While I didn't enjoy being ill, it became a way for me to survive and be released from some ugly situations when I was incarcerated.

I was not sexually abused during any of these detainments, but I was put to work on farms. Inmates were also sometimes asked to collect the dead bodies when there was an accident or natural disaster. Once we were asked to clean the mortuary without being given any protection from infections. It was like being a slave. In all of the prisons, there was no mattress, just a hard board shorter than my body. When I was required to lay down, I was not allowed to sleep on the floor. I had to lay with my head over the edge of the board. It was torturous.

The food we were given had no salt or preservatives, and it was hard on the stomach. The prisons I experienced were horrific, nothing like correctional facilities today in America. I recall going to speak at a prison in California

> I had given my life to telling my story for the Lord.

years ago where the prisoners were going on strike because they wanted cleaner facilities and better food (two pizzas a week) and other benefits. That shocked me. Those are luxuries for inmates in other countries today where they are truly in prison.

Whenever I was in custody and in pain, it just compelled me to pray that much more. I had given my life to telling my story for the Lord. I didn't care what happened. No matter what, I was going to continue doing what I was doing.

In college, I studied many subjects but focused mainly on my medical school training. I pursued my education in a way that I felt would help me bring forth the most healing to others in the future. This was done not so I could brag, but to recognize the grace of God and how He equipped me to make a difference for Him.

During those college years, I also took a two-year Bible correspondence course and began traveling outside of Africa to share my story in places such as Europe and the Middle East. I set up two locations from which I could manage my activities: a headquarters in Nairobi, Africa, and an operations center in Belfast, Northern Ireland. Every chance I got, I spoke to businesspeople or college chancellors, and I'd receive opportunities to speak from those meetings. I went wherever I could whenever I could, and I kept up my studies in the midst of it all.

I slept, but very briefly, usually a couple of hours a night and very lightly, like a rabbit sleeping with its eyes open. I'd later realize that the sleeplessness was an extension of my trauma. So many things had happened that if I thought about them too much or dreamed about them, I'd go crazy. So, in the hours I could've been sleeping, I stayed busy. I traveled, spoke, or studied. Instead of being a victim, I took my anger and the consequences of the traumas and used them positively, even if it wasn't the healthiest thing to do at the time.

Diverse people from places such as Ethiopia, Uganda, and Sudan began asking me to come to their countries to speak, and I started to create a database of contacts. This, in turn, generated opportunities for me to talk to government leaders on the topics of peace and reconciliation. I did this as often as I could, and as I built my network and went to different places, every event had its own beauty to it. When I was asked to go into southern Sudan to offer medical services and tell my story, it was to help bring reconciliation to various ethnic groups fighting one another in three different regions. Most of the men there were killed or recruited to go to war. The women and children were usually abducted, abused, and imprisoned. We met with elders, community authorities, and rebel leaders. We treated the wounded, and as I told my story, I used the Bible as often as I could, knowing that true reconciliation couldn't take place in people's hearts and minds without the Gospel of peace.

It was such a God-given opportunity to share, and it was lovely to see how many received the message of peace, love, and hope in Jesus. South Sudan became independent in 2011, but the country still sees conflict, with warring factions vying for power there to this day.

Of course, as I was able to go into those countries, there were times I'd meet with a specific side in an ethnic or political conflict, talk about reconciliation, and the opposing side didn't like it. Both sides felt like they couldn't trust me or that I was a spy, and for the most part, I was seen as the enemy. There were other cases when I'd speak out against something going on because I believed it was wicked. Some people don't want to hear that they need to repent and change.

I was sometimes detained for these reasons—but all of it began to inform what would eventually become the mission of what I do today through Unite 4 Africa: mobilize, unite, and equip individuals, communities, and organizations to transform themselves spiritually, socially, physically, and economically. We desire to see grassroots movements sweep across Africa and beyond, bringing abundant life in Christ to their people.

At most of these events I did not speak or preach from a podium or pulpit. They were intensive, two-hour-long interview formats, where a moderator asked questions and I answered them by telling stories about my experiences. It fit me so well because it exemplified the way Jesus talked to people. He taught through parables, and parables are stories drawn from real life.

I particularly love the story of the Prodigal Son in Luke 15:11-32. In it, a man had two sons. The younger son asked the father for his portion of the family estate as an early inheritance, and then embarked on a long journey to a distant land. He wasted his fortune on wild living, and when he was out of money, a severe famine came. The son took a job feeding pigs, and eventually became so desperate he wanted to eat the swine's food. When the son came to his senses, he recognized his foolishness and decided to return to his father to ask for forgiveness and mercy. The father, who had been watching and waiting for his son, received him with open arms, overjoyed by the return of his lost son. Not only did the father give grace and forgiveness to the son, but the son also recognized the sin he had done to the father.

The parable reminds me how we can so easily squander the many gifts we have been given by God and use them to do all sorts of sinful things against Him, yet still be received and loved by the Lord when we repent. It's the perfect scenario of grace that we can experience not only from God, but also from others that we have wronged or who have wronged us. It's the perfect message of forgiveness in Christ!

I find it interesting that most teachers of the story focus on the sins of the younger brother because his sins (sins of commission that he knowingly committed) were obvious. But there are two brothers in the account who were alienated from their father. There is no good or bad brother. Both needed redemption. The older brother's sins (sins of omission that he didn't knowingly commit) were in his self-righteous, bitter, and arrogant attitude. He wanted to be safe and good, but he failed to take any risks. He did not obey the self-care imperative of a godly older brother to seek a younger brother who was lost. Rather, he judged his brother and used that as an excuse to be distant. Yet he did not know his own sin, so he did not confess or repent and remained alienated from his father. I view the older brother as being like a religious person who is conforming but does not know the love of his Father in heaven. Trapped in rules, this person lacks a blessed life, failing to trust in a good God. I view the younger son as a worldly person who repents and is restored to relationship with God the Father.

I enjoyed telling my real-life parables in this way. The interview format was necessary to accommodate for the language barrier between me and my audiences, and the moderator often served as interpreter. I talked to thousands of people at a time, and it gave me a chance to connect with and captivate them. In addition, I hosted small group storytelling gatherings.

During my time in college and over the next several years, I can't recall how many times I spoke. It was like an addiction. It was meat and drink to me. In each and every place, I chose a different story to fit with the country, the audience, or both. For example, when I went somewhere with a Muslim background, I emphasized how God rescued me from abduction or prison, and I chose Bible passages declaring God as a God of deliverance. I recall sharing the story of Moses speaking to the Israelites in Exodus 14:13-14. Moses told them, "Do not be afraid. Stand firm and you will see the deliverance the Lord will bring you today. The Egyptians you see today you will never see again. The Lord will fight for you; you need only to be still." God then imparted to Moses the wisdom to lead the people safely through the Red Sea as God supernaturally parted the waters for them.

The message to not fear, be strong, and remain in the Lord often challenged my faith when I was incarcerated, terrified, and not certain that God would save me at all. It was easier to doubt and give in to my fear. But I came to trust in that message and in Him. I discovered that this story resonated with a majority of my Muslim audiences, but I used it with other groups as well. All of them appreciated that I was telling it from the perspective of someone who had been imprisoned many times yet showed that God could rescue them from any situation.

Another teaching that was important to me came from Matthew 7:1-5. In it, Jesus taught us not to judge others. I had been judged throughout my young life, even before I was abducted and escaped from the LRA. I experienced the judgment of others when I taught. Yet I also had to be careful to not judge them as well. I had to remove the plank from my eye so that I could see them and love them as Jesus did and serve them as He intended. It was, and continues to be, a powerful teaching in my life, and it helps me to not act like the older brother in the story of the Prodigal Son.

If I spoke to a group of Christian leaders who already knew Christ as Lord, I shared how I was marginalized by Christians in authority after I was kidnapped. I challenged them that we, as believers in God, must do better by lifting people up, not beating them down. Again, I chose Scripture to go along with the message, such as when Jesus spoke to the Scribes and Pharisees about their hypocrisy, impacting some of the people in those audiences the same way Jesus did the priests and teachers of the law in His day.

When I am invited to speak, I want to first know the background of that place or audience and what is going on in that community. That way, I can trust the Lord to show me what He wants me to share and what ministers to them the most. I often had opportunities to talk directly with audience members before or after my presentations. I discovered that most of those who wished to meet me personally had been through some sort of trauma in their own lives—trauma they had never shared with anyone else until they met me. They had always felt inferior, timid, or afraid to declare what had happened to them. But hearing me tell my story inspired them to have the courage to share their wounds and seek healing.

One such person was a lady I met outside a refugee camp in Northern Kenya who was gang raped and didn't get help from her family. I thought it was profound and sad how she was still dealing with what had happened without anyone else knowing or caring. Because she had given birth to a child as a result of the assault and did not know who the father was, she was silenced and excommunicated by her family and community. They felt she had been possessed by an evil spirit and was mentally ill. The woman was stigmatized and a true outcast.

It was by accident that she heard me speak that evening, in that she wasn't a refugee and wasn't even supposed to be there. After she told me her story, I wept and prayed for her. Others in the group with me joined in, and God healed her! Instantly, she was transformed by God's Holy Spirit. It was amazing to see someone who had only known rejection be loved, accepted, and redeemed by the Lord. Even though she feared further rejection and other negative and potentially harmful consequences from sharing her story, she was still determined to praise God for setting her free! Because of what happened to me at the hands of the LRA, I understood her experience, fear, and risk of rejection better than most.

Today, I often minister to those who, like that woman, are thought to be clinically mentally ill when, really, they are harshly wounded by the traumas they are mentally carrying around with them. I will share my story, then talk to them to bring out their story. As I do, the Lord helps them take my story into account, acknowledge and accept their own situation, and then take humble steps to release their trust and reconcile themselves to Him. I met a man in his twenties who, when rebels in Sudan invaded his village as a child, had watched as his mother was raped and his parents were killed. He was severely traumatized and wondered why he wasn't killed as well. He developed mental, emotional, and psychological issues that caused him to be unhealthy and hurt others around him. It wasn't easy, but God enabled me to minister to him, and the Lord has delivered and restored him. Today, he is serving people as a pastor in South Sudan—and my faith in God grows as I see Him work in the lives of people that are like he was when I worked with him. It's incredible!

I attended a convention organized by the United Nations High Commissioner which was helping refugees (internally displaced persons, also known as IDPs) who were being moved from one country to another. While there, I was told that help was especially needed in Yemen. They arranged for me to fly to Sana'a, the capital of Yemen, in the same medical roles as before so that I could learn more about the nature of the conflict there, seek reconciliation, and help the IDP's through their trauma. Some of them had seen their families tortured and murdered.

As I did this, I also facilitated the start of small underground gatherings where I could tell people about the Bible and Christ. However, word spread quickly about these groups, and after just a month in Yemen, I was summoned by the religious leaders there and asked about what I was doing. I told them I was simply sharing my story, being careful to not mention how I was including the teachings of Scripture in my messaging. I was still found guilty, not of spreading the religion of Christianity itself, but of tampering with the Islamic culture of the country. I was imprisoned and ended up behind bars for two-and-a-half months. While incarcerated, I started similar small groups within the prison itself. That became such a problem, I was let go earlier than expected.

When I was released, I was no worse for wear except for the 39 lashes I received. Seven of those lashes were delivered in a public gathering outside the prison as a way of shaming me and setting a "no tolerance" example for other potential cultural offenders. I was given two choices: stay in the country and serve the people as I had been, without sharing my faith or having underground meetings, or be deported out of the country. I chose to stay—in part because I was confused about where to go next, but also because, despite my wounds, I loved seeing what God was doing in the hearts of the people. It would've been easier to leave, and my choice shocked even me, but I continued to serve in Yemen. I kept sharing my faith, too, with the small groups who, at great risk to themselves from fear of being discovered, still gathered in the early hours of the morning, usually right after midnight. I just didn't get caught again.

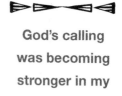

There was a mighty move of God happening; people were being touched by my messages and wanted to seek Him. In addition, many were impressed that I didn't leave, seeing that as a confirmation of the validity

God's calling was becoming stronger in my heart.

of God's love for them, and of what He was doing in Yemen. More than once, people told me, "You were humiliated. You were put in prison. You were given lashes, and you chose not to leave. This, then, is not about you." One man, who later became a Christian, took the thought even further, saying, "If it was about you, you would've left." I enjoyed so many more moments of the Lord's compassion and healing power I otherwise would've missed had I decided to leave the country.

I couldn't help myself. God's calling was becoming stronger in my heart. I wasn't acting according to how I felt, but I was compelled by what He was telling me to do.

After all the pain and humiliation, it would've been easy for me to give in, give up, and leave. But it wasn't about how I felt. I was learning that God's Word and His will for my life superseded my feelings—and I had to share the Gospel, no matter what.

Yet there remained a struggle within my heart and soul. It was still difficult at times to trust God. In many ways, it was easier for me to trust Him with the lives of others than to believe Him for my own healing. The trauma from my own experiences continued to haunt me. At times, I did not feel adequate or that I was doing enough when others resisted what I did or when they did not respond positively. Claims from some church leaders that it wasn't God, but me, who told me to go into Uganda before my abduction echoed in my mind like mocking whispers. Their judgment of me warred with my ability to accept myself as I was.

Then there was the fear that the next time I got arrested somewhere, I might not get out alive. I had seen people die in prison.

I became more depressed and anxious beyond what anyone else could imagine. There were still times I wanted to quit, moments where I refused to even listen to what His Word told me was true. Yet despite my inner and outer wounds, my love for people and my desire to honor His call were strong and kept me going.

Honoring His call was bigger than me.

Not long after my imprisonment in Yemen, I met a group of social workers and teachers from Saudi Arabia and other Middle Eastern countries at a monthly meeting of expatriates done at the invitation of local authorities. Even though they weren't Christians (some expatriates were secretly religious missionaries who did other jobs, such as being a doctor or teacher, so they could go into countries they otherwise would not be allowed to enter), they wanted me to come to Saudi Arabia.

I wondered why. I was obviously not originally from the Middle East. They had heard about my story and my recent public whipping outside the prison from other expatriates who likely witnessed the beating. My belief in God was obvious. They were not believers.

But they still asked me to go, and I did not want to miss the opportunity. I had no doubt that it was Jesus who was making the way.

It would be in Saudi Arabia where I was going to face my most trying and painful imprisonment yet—one that would call my very faith in God into question.

Chapter 3

TORTURE, DENIAL, AND REDEMPTION

When I had the opportunity to visit Saudi Arabia the first time, I was able to visit with all the individuals I'd met in Yemen and their friends who were interested in learning more about me. As a black man from Africa, I was not only seen as different; I was considered inferior. Most everywhere I went outside of Africa, others struggled to believe that I could be so well educated. They wanted to marginalize me, and this was especially true when I was in the Middle East.

Yet I earned the respect of my various hosts as I shared with them what I did. As a medical missionary, I found out what was making people sick, did diagnosis and research, and provided treatment. I came against the misconceptions and superstitions most people had about their illnesses and changed their mindset about why they were sick and how to get better. I assisted and empowered medical professionals who were already in the countries I visited.

The Saudis also wanted to know why I was so passionate about what I was doing to help others, and how that passion tied to my faith. Since they were Muslim, I reminded them of my story, the one they had first heard about when they were in Yemen. We also talked about my views on a variety of other issues including, of course, religion. I didn't hide the call I felt God had given me to love others for Jesus, and I told them how I became a believer in Christ.

When I was finished, they came to a fascinating conclusion: based on what I said and did, they felt I should become a Muslim. They wanted me to believe and accept that the holy prophet Muhammad was the last prophet of Allah; specifically, that Muhammad was the one Jesus had said would come after Him as a helper or counselor (not the Holy Spirit, as Christians believe).

The moment anyone recognizes the prophet Muhammad as the last prophet, they are considered to be a Muslim. But I didn't accept Muhammad, and the more I disagreed with that, the more disappointed and upset they became. Still, over my two weeks there, I looked to network and create other connections and relationships. While I encountered skepticism, there were others who were secretly interested and wanted to know more.

I was also warned quite clearly about the consequences I could face if I continued to share my story and my faith in Saudi Arabia—and that those consequences would be unpleasant.

When I left Saudi Arabia, I was determined to return as soon as I could. From there, I went to Egypt and then back to Kenya to rest before going back to Yemen and finally making the follow-up trip back to Saudi Arabia. In all, about two months passed between the first and second visits.

When I returned, I was hosted by the people I connected with on my first trip, friends of those who had hosted me the first time. I did not do medical work, or any other occupational task for that matter. I didn't have any papers providing an actual reason for me to be in the country. When asked, I said I was there to learn the Najdi Arabic language, which was different from the Juba Arabic I'd learned in Sudan. I knew being able to speak the native language well would make me more accepted and welcome. In fact, in the Islamic culture, learning Arabic is like learning Islam itself since they consider Arabic to be the language of Allah. If you speak Arabic, they think it's because you are trying to get closer to Allah. I was also interested in them as a people and in their culture. I even wanted to see how they worshipped and prayed, joining them in their mosques. Even though that confused some people because they thought that by going into the mosques I had become a Muslim, I still thought it was the right thing to do. I was modeling what Jesus had done. He went to the house of the sinner. To be where people are is a God-given strategy.

Everywhere I went, I followed Christ's guidance from Matthew 10:11, which says, "Whatever town or village you enter, search there for some worthy person and stay at their house until you leave." In Scripture, I think of the woman at the well (John 4), Cornelius (Acts 10), and Lydia (Acts 16) as examples of those God chose and helped as they aided His messenger. I looked for the "worthy person" who would welcome me, people of peace who were there as a result of God's intervention in their life, and often they came to me. I identified these people as I prayed for them and asked God to give me discernment about them.

When I interacted with these worthy people in Saudi Arabia, I did everything I could to tell them how God was my rescuer, redeemer, and Savior. As I met with people (mostly men; Islamic culture is rigidly segregated between men and women) in places where they gathered in public such as markets or community events, I was asked what was going through my mind, particularly when I was in prison in Yemen, and why I was arrested in an Islamic country—and I boldly told them. Whenever I was invited into homes where people gathered for tea and women could be present, I shared what God had laid in my heart and how I had tried to be faithful to His calling. I said that it was only through God that a person like me could come to Saudi Arabia in the first place. I then transitioned into telling them why I was in Saudi Arabia: to declare that Jesus had died for us.

In a given day, I could tell several stories because in every gathering there was a different audience and I spoke to them in a different way. Because I was in Saudi Arabia, I avoided carrying around my Bible, and I told stories that I had memorized from Scripture. That was easy for me because of the oral culture I come from where storytelling was a big part of life. I told the stories in my own words, and then began a dialogue about it by asking questions to learn what they understood. That often prompted them to tell me stories from their own lives.

Before sharing a story with people, I first engaged in a simple conversation to get to know them and establish a dialogue. That allowed me to then discern what story from the Bible fit best for that group. I'd ask them to tell me about their lives and their families, and they'd ask about mine. This process showed incredible respect, established relationship, and developed trust.

One time I was speaking to a group of Saudi men, and one asked, "I hear in Africa they marry more than four wives. Here, according to Islam, we are only allowed to marry up to four." That allowed me to begin a conversation about marriage and tell them a story showing how men and women are to love and respect one another using principles from Genesis, Ephesians, and Colossians.

It was all about taking every opportunity to have a dialogue that led back to the biblical perspective on that subject. Again, that is how Jesus did it when He spoke to the crowds using parables (Mark 4:34). Christ always related to His audience, and I tried to do the same.

I declared the love and salvation of Christ.

I had come back to Saudi Arabia to build more new relationships, share my story and the love of God, and to establish new followers of Jesus in that country.

It was exactly what I had been told could have unpleasant consequences.

As I did all of this, I knew I was showing disrespect to the Islamic culture, which was an offense. There were many who disagreed with my philosophy and my faith, knowing that I was not embracing the belief that the prophet Muhammad was the last prophet of Allah. Some asserted that I was speaking a teaching or ideology that contradicted what Islam was teaching and disrespected the teaching of the holy prophet Muhammad. This put me in the place of being an outsider.

A false teacher. An infidel.

This eventually led to me being questioned by the Islamic religious police (The Committee for the Promotion of Virtue and the Prevention of Vice, also referred to as the Mutaween). They are tasked with enforcing conservative Islamic norms of public behavior as defined by Saudi authorities—and they wanted to know why I was in the country and who had allowed me to come or given me permission to be there.

Through the Mutaween, I got into trouble—and I was detained.

"Do you believe that the holy prophet Muhammad, peace be upon him, is the holy, last prophet," they demanded, "that he is the messenger of the living god, Allah?"

"No," I replied. "It is Jesus. We receive salvation through Jesus who died on the cross and rose from the dead on the third day."

I became an enemy the moment I said that. To some Muslims, it is a fabrication that Christ died and rose again.

The prophet must be respected.

Sad but true, anything less is unforgiven. Nothing else matters.

I was found guilty of disrespecting the holy prophet Muhammad, destabilizing the culture, bringing distorted religion, and inciting public opinion.

I was thrown into prison.

I was given a six-year sentence with lashes to be administered daily.

Little did I realize there was going to be more punishment than that—much more.

I was taken to Al-Ha'ir—which today is a maximum-security prison located about 25 miles south of Riyadh. Saudi Arabia's largest prison, the complex is spread out over a barren desert plain and includes facilities for both common criminals and security offenders, and it reportedly houses a number of al-Qaeda figures.

Like other prisons in Saudi Arabia at that time, Al-Ha'ir was extremely bad. It had no set routine or schedule. The food was basic but certainly acceptable: eggs, beans, rice, and chicken. I'd had worse elsewhere. Though our toilet was just a hole in the ground, the water was good because water purity is valued in the Islamic faith. They even made us wash our hands often.

Because of the nature of my offense, my lashes started the very first day. I was interrogated quite a bit the first few days of my incarceration. I think they were trying to find out if I had more of a network within Saudi Arabia or if I had some outside sources trying to support me. While I certainly didn't like the questioning, I didn't let it deter me. Because I was considered a maximum-security inmate, I was initially placed in a large room with other prisoners. That allowed me to talk to and connect with some of the other inmates. As we spoke Najdi Arabic to one another, God used it to help me learn the language—but I also looked for opportunities to share.

> I continued to tell my story and the love and salvation of Christ.

I continued to tell my story and the love and salvation of Christ. I did the same with those who could speak English.

It wasn't allowed, but I did it anyway.

Even more, I was actually glad to be there because I could interact with the other prisoners and do what God had called me to do.

My persistence, though, only got me into more trouble. I was relocated to more isolated confinement where I was held captive with fewer prisoners, but I only shared more. I sang, worshipped, and prayed to God.

That resulted in more punishment. I was suspended from the ceiling by my wrists. They were cuffed in steel shackles that painfully dug into my skin as the full weight of my body pulled me downward. As I hung there, I knew my captors wanted me to be quiet. I promised them I'd stop speaking and singing, and I was lowered. Yet, after the pain subsided, I resumed what I had been doing.

Electrical shock was then added to my torture. I was forced to sit in a chair, and then wires were attached directly to my skin. The shock treatments caused intense muscle pain, full-body seizures and contractions, and made it difficult to breathe. They usually rendered me unconscious. I felt like I was going to die, yet each time I recovered and realized I was still alive. I didn't want them to do it again.

Still, after a day or two, I'd rebel once again. I spoke about my God and Jesus as the Savior. I sang about Him.

Then I was shown a horrifying needle. It had a hook on the end and jagged teeth along its razor-sharp edge. I was told that if I didn't shut up, my lips would be sewn shut using that needle.

After seeing that freaking needle, I did not want to even open my mouth to eat. It truly frightened me like nothing else I'd seen or experienced to that point. I stayed quiet—for a bit. Eventually, my fears would subside, and I'd again speak or sing.

So, it went. It seemed like I was getting lashes every second. My pain and agony were constant. Each day might as well have been a year.

Yet I didn't stop. My voice would not be silenced. My hope would not be quenched.

Then I was led into the room where I'd been hung from the ceiling, and I was interrogated once more.

"Do you believe Jesus Christ is not the Son of God?" My captor began yelling. "He cannot be the Son! He cannot be God! He cannot be the Savior! He cannot be the Holy Spirit!"

I would not recant.

Others entered the room, forced me to the floor, and held me down. I desperately tried to resist, but I was so weak, I couldn't.

Vrewww. Vrewww.

I heard the unmistakable sound of a power drill.

Felt the calves of my legs being pressed hard into the ground.

Screamed in blinding agony as the drill bit spun into my skin, penetrated through flesh, muscle, and sinew, and punctured my tibia, down close to my ankle.

First one leg, and then the other.

I slammed my eyes shut. Tears streamed. At some point, I became deaf to my own cries.

I'd never known such pain.

I opened my eyes and looked down just long enough to see my captors grab a steel rod, and I had no question of their intention for it.

The cold steel cruelly snaked its way through the burrow created in both of my legs. Warm blood gushed. I could literally hear its moist release from my body.

As I bordered on unconsciousness, I felt my body rising into the air upside down. I realized the bar piercing my legs was being hoisted up toward the ceiling by chains that had been fastened to each side.

I dangled there like a slab of freshly butchered meat. That's what I was.

Blood rushed to my head, and the darkness came.

I don't know how long I hung there or how long I was unconscious. But when I came to, I was back on the ground and the rod was no longer in my legs.

Pain penetrated my entire being.

The same captor who had yelled at me earlier asked once more, quieter but determined.

"Do you accept Jesus Christ is not the Savior and the Son of God?"

That's when it happened.

"I agree!" I screamed. "Muhammad is the holy, last prophet of God!"

As I began to cry, I was carried to a room where I was placed in solitary confinement. My body trembled, but ever so slowly, the pain started to fade.

Not that it mattered any longer.

I am going to die.

I was convinced of it. Then another thought, almost comical, entered my mind.

That must be why they never sewed my mouth shut. They wanted me to confess.

I had—but it wasn't a genuine confession. I'd said it in fear. To stop the torture. To keep myself from again being skewered and hung.

I had denied Jesus Christ with my words.

But I still clung to Him in my heart.

Fresh tears flowed, and the next words I formed and spoke, only as a whimpering whisper, were from the chorus of a song by Ray Boltz.

"I pledge allegiance to the Lamb. With all my strength, with all I am. I will seek to honor His commands. I pledge allegiance to the Lamb."

It wasn't lost on me how the lyrics of that incredible song spoke of Christians long ago being brought before a tyrant's throne and told their lives would be spared if they renounced the name of Christ.

One by one, they had chosen to die.

I hadn't.

All I could do was believe that Jesus knew the intent of my heart—and that He would forgive me.

That was all I had.

I was going to die anyway.

I wanted to die praising and worshipping the Lord.

How long after that—hours, days, I don't know—my incarceration ended. I was supposed to have stayed at Al-Ha'ir for six years—but, in the end, I was released after about a month.

I was never told why, but I believe I was removed from prison early not just because of my confession, but because I was at the point of death.

I wasn't dead yet, but I might as well have been.

The torture and mutilation had taken their toll. I was ravaged physically, emotionally, and spiritually.

It turned out everyone had been right all along.

The consequences were more than unpleasant.

To this day, and likely until the day I die, I regret denying Christ. It bothers me that I waivered. It always reminds me that, even though we are forgiven by God for our past actions, there are some actions that will always cause us to feel guilty and experience regret. We are not under condemnation for those actions anymore. Romans 8:1 is clear that "there is now no condemnation for those who are in Christ Jesus." But this kind of guilt is good guilt—the type of sorrow that keeps us on the

> To this day, and likely until the day I die, I regret denying Christ.

path of obedience to God and reminds us of His amazing grace and mercy towards us. As 2 Corinthians 7:10 says, "Godly sorrow brings repentance that leads to salvation and leaves no regret, but worldly sorrow brings death."

When I was released from prison, I wasn't able to walk, and I suspected I had an infection or worse because my leg bones had been drilled, but I wasn't taken to a hospital. Rather, I was released into the custody of a Muslim Imam named Sheikh Nasser. I later realized I was kept in his home next to a mosque, but I was not told then what was going on. Even when I was carried on a stretcher to the Imam's residence, I thought it was probably just another part of the prison. While I was recovering, I thought that once I was healed, I was going back to jail. I did not know if I was really released or not.

Today, Sheikh Nasser is my good friend, and I have utmost respect for him because he brought people in to treat my wounds and help nurse me back to health. But make no mistake, the first several days I was under his care, I still thought I was going to die. I was in such pain I couldn't differentiate between day or night. As my awareness slowly grew, I realized I was being cleaned up each morning before Muslim prayers. I was guided to the bathroom, and those taking care of me even washed me afterward because I was unable to clean myself. I was given good, nutritious food. They were gracious and loving as they took care of me, even as they offered prayers over me.

Yet I struggled to trust any of those men. I sometimes believed the good food was only temporary, or that tomorrow they'd just kill me because I was too much of a burden for them. I thought only the worst. I was still very afraid and uncertain because of everything I had been through the past month or so.

I believe the Imam was under the impression that I was progressing and being converted to the Muslim faith. In truth, I was still worshipping God in my heart. The graciousness of the Lord was truly amazing to me.

I had made it. I was alive.

Much more, I knew God had forgiven me.

In all, I was with the sheikh for over three weeks. A few days into my stay, most of the few belongings I had when I went into Al-Ha'ir were brought to me—except for my journals, schedule book, and my Bible. The most significant moment in my time with the Imam came about a week after that when I was taken to his study room. It was big, about the size of a bedroom, but it didn't have any chairs, so I was laid out on a mat.

As I looked around, I noticed that Sheikh Nasser had a Bible on his bookshelf.

I was surprised, but I later discovered that most Muslim Imams possess a Bible and have knowledge of the Scriptures.

As was my usual practice, I initiated a conversation.

"I see you have the Bible, which is what I was reading," I said. He then told me why he had the Bible, and how that particular Bible was in English as well as Arabic. "It is a good, godly book," he said.

"I can speak Arabic," I told him in Najdi, "but I cannot read Arabic at this time. Could I borrow your Bible and read it?"

"Oh, yes. You are welcome," he said.

He had no hesitance. He surely thought I was asking to read it as part of my efforts to become a Muslim.

I couldn't believe it. I was so happy. I returned with it to my room, and I immediately turned to Romans 8. I started with those precious words my soul longed to hear again—"Therefore, there is now no condemnation for those who are in Christ Jesus"—and read on, focusing on verses 28-39.

"And we know that in all things God works for the good of those who love him, who have been called according to his purpose. For those God foreknew he also predestined to be conformed to the image of his Son, that he might be the firstborn among many brothers and sisters. And those he predestined, he also called; those he called, he also justified; those he justified, he also glorified."

Verses 28-30 reminded me that God works *all things* for good. I thought of my imprisonment and of the tortures I'd endured. Were they part of "all things?" They were. Now, I was being fed and washed, and treated for my injuries. I was sick and helpless, yet God had made a way for me to get help and be well again. Only He could do that! My heart leaped as I considered anew the fact that I had gone through everything for His purposes. In fact, God had called me for this purpose from the very beginning.

I read on under the section titled "More Than Conquerors."

"What, then, shall we say in response to these things? If God is for us, who can be against us? He who did not spare his own Son, but gave him up for us all—how will he not also, along with him, graciously give us all things?"

That passage, verses 31-32, told me that nothing and no one could be against me because Christ was *for* me! Even people who were not aligned with my faith were being used by God at that very moment to take care of me. It was incredible!

I continued, tears coming to my eyes.

"Who will bring any charge against those whom God has chosen? It is God who justifies. Who then is the one who condemns? No one. Christ Jesus who died—more than that, who was raised to life—is at the right hand of God and is also interceding for us. Who shall separate us from the love of Christ? Shall trouble or hardship or persecution or famine or nakedness or danger or sword? As it is written: 'For your sake we face death all day long; we are considered as sheep to be slaughtered.'"

Verses 33-36 confirmed that God had been there for me and

with me, in good times or bad, not only in Saudi Arabia, but ever since I had become a believer. I also realized that all the way back to when I was abducted by the LRA, and in every situation since then, Jesus had been *interceding* for me. He was at the right-hand side of God praying to the Father on my behalf.

At that moment, few people knew where I was. I had not been given time to let people know what had happened before I was arrested. Communication technologies such as smartphones, texting, and social media did not exist back then. Therefore, I didn't have a group of people praying for me.

But Jesus was, and that meant God knew where I was. I was also reminded of the Great Commission from Matthew 28:19-20 and the wonderful words of encouragement at the close of the passage. "Therefore go and make disciples of all nations, baptizing them in the name of the Father and of the Son and of the Holy Spirit, and teaching them to obey everything I have commanded you. And surely I am with you always, to the very end of the age."

Then I completed my amazing time in Romans 8 with verses 37-39.

"No, in all these things we are more than conquerors through him who loved us. For I am convinced that neither death nor life, neither angels nor demons, neither the present nor the future, nor any powers, neither height nor depth, nor anything else in all creation, will be able to separate us from the love of God that is in Christ Jesus our Lord."

Wow! No trouble or hardship or persecution or famine or nakedness or danger or sword—nothing—could separate me from the love of Christ! His love for me was *great!* More than that, He had not forsaken me, even after I had denied Him with my words.

Once again, I couldn't breathe, but it wasn't from electrocution. It was from the renewed understanding of my Lord's love for me. It literally took my breath away.

Not only did I know that I was still a Christian, but I knew that I was *His*.

I belonged to God—and I always would.

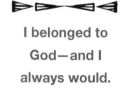

I belonged to God—and I always would.

Eventually, the Islamic religious police came to see me at Sheikh Nasser's home, and they were apparently pleased with what they saw. They wanted to make sure that, in their eyes, I was following through on my confession to become a Muslim.

I was then told I was going to be deported. To where I had no idea.

Even as final preparations were made and I was taken to the airport, I still thought the worst. *Sure, I was well enough to get around on crutches, but what difference does it make? I'm just going to another prison. To more torture. To someplace else to die.*

I thought it was all a cruel joke.

Until I was safely on the plane, and I found out where it was going.

Chapter 4

FROM TRAUMA TO DELIVERANCE

The destination, Malaysia, was not my choice. It was what the deportation required. Yet when I arrived, I was free.

But I struggled to believe it.

Despite the encouragement I'd read in God's Word while I was with Sheikh Nasser, I remained psychologically wounded. I was experiencing something similar to post-traumatic stress disorder. It was like I had been through a war. My mind needed time for God's healing process to begin and for me to recover. I wasn't okay mentally, emotionally, or spiritually—and I still didn't know where I was going next.

That is often the way the Lord works in our lives. It's His timing that counts. But that reality still didn't comfort me.

I was in Malaysia for two days, the entire time in the custody of airport security. My next flight took me to the United Arab Emirates, where I'd spend another two days at the airport there. Physically, I was limited and slow, a carryover of the many injuries I sustained at Al-Ha'ir. I kept to myself, mired in anger, anxiety, and depression. I still couldn't help but wonder if I was heading to another prison and more torture. The only thing I knew for sure was that I was still alive. But despair continued to engulf me.

From there, I was taken to London, England and another full day at Heathrow Airport before I was placed on my final flight.

It took me home.

To Kenya.

I was actually disappointed. I had assumed I was going to be flown to nearby Northern Ireland, where my operating center was located in Belfast. I saw that as my base and a bit of a hiding place, a quiet spot where no one was going to ask questions I did not want to answer when I really didn't know what was going on with me. I thought I'd have more opportunity to rest and recover there, more than I would at my headquarters in Africa.

The location of my operations in Nairobi was at a home in the Pangani Estate neighborhood where up to six people stayed at a time. They were there either because they had come to the city looking for a job or were visiting someone and needed a place to stay. Africa is communal. There are always people around.

No one knew I was coming, of course, so no one met me at the airport in Nairobi. When I arrived at the home after 11:00 p.m., the people who were there knew I had been to the Middle East. But they were used to me being away for long periods of time, so my arrival was nothing unusual. I wasn't carrying my usual pair of travel bags, but only a single smaller bag with the meager possessions I was provided when I left Saudi Arabia. Since I was struggling to walk, it was obvious that something bad had happened to me, and they likely assumed that I had been beaten or robbed, an all-too-often occurrence there. Therefore, they didn't ask many questions, and I settled in as best I could.

Still, news of my return spread quickly, and others started dropping by to visit during the day. That took away some of the time alone that I desperately needed, and I just wasn't ready yet to share the ugly story of what had actually happened to me in Saudi Arabia.

Despite the distractions, I tried to take more time to heal, but my struggles continued, especially at night. My body, especially my leg bones, were still healing, and they were quite sore. Consequently, standing up or lying down were both painful experiences. That just made me angrier.

Why me? I lamented. *Why did I have to go through that? They could have killed me so I wouldn't have to be here living in shame.* I again relived my denial of Christ, and the condemnation I thought was gone returned. I didn't need someone else to shame me for what I did. I shamed myself over and over.

Then I began to grieve, feeling I had lost my sense of direction and purpose. I was depressed because, since I'd been taken to Kenya instead of Northern Ireland, I couldn't get to my assets in my bank in Belfast. I like to have a plan, and I want things to go as scheduled. When that doesn't happen, I typically get upset. With all that going on, my desperate need to heal mentally, emotionally, and physically was becoming even more critical. I didn't want to reschedule all my plans. I wanted to go forward.

As I tried to cope with the seriousness of my situation, my longtime friend, Gordon, took care of me. The key person who oversaw the logistics of my activities, he picked up my self-prescribed medications and bought and brought home groceries and other supplies I needed. His sister, Dorothy, came by often to cook for us. At the same time, other people came by to help, not necessarily because I had been in prison and was still healing, but because it was what they would normally do for a leader or the provider of a household.

That meant a great deal to me. I was in great need, and their kindness, compassion, and acts of service were so compelling in the midst of my physical and mental distress.

Yet even their care and concern weren't enough to prevent the trauma I'd endured in Saudi Arabia from returning. In fact, it took me back to every other trauma I'd experienced in the past, all the way back to my abduction by the LRA. I experienced flashbacks of the kidnapping, rapes, and the harrowing escape, of the other imprisonment and lashes, and of course, of the horrific tortures at Al-Ha'ir. With each one, as vivid and real as though I was again going through them, negative thoughts assailed me.

Why did I go through that? How did I escape that? Why did God abandon me?

My shame, depression, anxiety, and questions increased.

Each pain of the past was like a new pain—and each new pain was a failure. Even though I had a clear understanding of God's grace, the pain was so great, it seemed too big a challenge to overcome.

Each pain of the past was like a new pain.

All I felt was failure.

In my devastation, I'd go for short walks into the Mathare slum neighborhood located just east of the house in Pangani. It was a destitute place where gangsters roamed with machetes and people being beaten was common, but it was also where I could view English Premier League football matches on satellite TV. I enjoyed watching matches with my beloved Manchester United. They provided a few moments of peace. I knew it was always risky to go into the slums. There was a very real chance I could be attacked or killed on my way back home at night—but I often welcomed the thought.

Why don't they kill me? That would be the easiest way to deal with this pain.

It would be a way to die without actually committing suicide.

To my disappointment, no one tried to take my life, so I decided to press the issue by openly confronting the gangsters. Once, after one of them had just used his machete to hack someone, I stepped right up to him.

"What you are doing is wrong! God will judge you!"

Yes, I suppose I was presenting the gospel, although I was mostly hoping to provoke him. I was doing everything I could to be aggressive. *If he chops off my head, I thought, that's fine with me.* That was how deeply the hopelessness had penetrated my being.

Yet even then, in my twisted and perverse mindset, God showed Himself to me. He wasn't going to allow them to take my life. He said, "Never will I leave you; never will I forsake you." (Hebrew 13:5) I had my own plan for the ruthless slum gangsters, but He instead used my misplaced boldness to actually show His love for them through me.

Every time I'd return home unharmed, I'd wonder, *Why didn't they kill me? What is wrong?*

God dealt with me in a way that drew me closer to Him while simultaneously inflaming my anger toward Him. *If I can die, the pain will go away. If I can die, I will never have to talk about this. If I can die, I would go where the other disciples and apostles who were killed as a result of the gospel had gone.*

If I could die, I could go on to peace.

I craved that release. I wanted to run from the pain.

I wanted my life to end.

But God simply wouldn't allow my life to be taken.

As I battled myself and God, it renewed my doubts about what I was doing and even about who I was. As I had done ever since I'd become a Christian, I went back to the Bible. I started reading from Genesis all the way to Revelation—and all along the way, I discovered there were scriptures that pointed toward my healing.

The book of 2 Kings 20 was very personal. One of the kings of Judah, Hezekiah, was so ill he was at the point of death. Then the Lord said, "I have heard your prayer and seen your tears; I will heal you. On the third day from now you will go up to the temple of the Lord." (verse 5) When I read that, I thought, *That is mine. God can hear my prayer if I pray for Him to heal me.* I began to pray more, aloud and in my heart, believing that if I could pray the next three days, or four days, or ten, I could hope that God would hear me.

Yet I was also hopeless. Doubt warred against my optimism.

I was starting to trust God, but I also wavered in that trust.

I moved ahead in the Bible to the Psalms and came across Psalm 6:2, written by David, the most well-known king of Israel and Judah. "Have pity on me, O Lord, because I am weak. Heal me, O Lord, because my bones shake with terror." (GW) When I read that, it was as real as could be. At times, my bones were so painful at night, they trembled. I wondered why David said his bones felt that way. *Could it be that he went through what I went through?* Then I considered how God was the one who called me and sent me to those places where I was tortured. *Well, I am believing your Word. You led me there. Healing is from you. I need you to heal me.*

I progressed to Proverbs 17:22. "A cheerful heart is good medicine, but a crushed spirit dries up the bones." *If I am not cheerful*, I reasoned, *then my spirit is dry. What can I do to be cheerful?* People who know me today say I come across joyful and so happy, and it's because that scripture became a point of healing for me. It was medicine to my soul. Not only am I able to find joy in God during times of great difficulty, pain, and even loss, but even during odd situations such as when I accidentally hit my finger with a hammer while working on a construction project. Through the Lord, I can be easily cheerful, no matter what I come up against in my life.

The next passage that gave me comfort was Isaiah 41:10. God declared, "Do not fear, for I am with you; do not be dismayed, for I am your God." What a powerful message that was in my fearful moments. The verse continued, "I will strengthen you and help you; I will uphold you with my righteous right hand." *God, you sent me to all those places, and here I am. You are still my God, yet I am dismayed.* I started to develop more faith.

I kept on reading, proceeding to the book of Jeremiah, written by a man commonly known as "the weeping prophet." In Jeremiah 17:14, he said, "Heal me, Lord, and I will be healed; save me and I will be saved, for you are the one I praise." Biblical prophets like Jeremiah cried out to the Lord, and that was the source of their healing. I realized that my healing needed to go beyond what I could perceive as a doctor, past the prescriptions written by men. My healing needed to come from the Lord. I needed God to save me from my trauma, fear, and unhappiness, and I could receive that by praising Him.

Wow! I could have died in Yemen, Saudi Arabia, Sudan—in all of those places. But I am alive. Yes, I'm in pain, but there is something I can do: praise Him! God, I want to praise you in the middle of my pain. I want to thank you because you saved me.

I needed to acknowledge that by praising Him, I would receive healing.

As I meditated on Jeremiah's plea, I recalled the Apostle Paul's words from 1 Thessalonians 5:16-24. "Rejoice always, pray continually, give thanks in all circumstances; for this is God's will for you in Christ Jesus. Do not quench the Spirit. Do not treat

God, I want to praise you in the middle of my pain.

prophecies with contempt but test them all; hold on to what is good, reject every kind of evil. May God himself, the God of peace, sanctify you through and through. May your whole spirit, soul and body be kept blameless at the coming of our Lord Jesus Christ. The one who calls you is faithful, and he will do it."

Give thanks in all circumstances? I thought. *Really?* That was not easy, but in obedience to God's Word, I knew I had to do it. I needed my belief to come against my disbelief. During moments when I was in intense pain, I sometimes thought that the prophets and disciples were nutcases, but I reminded myself that their words were inspired by God, and I felt comfort as I kept reading. *Rejoice? Continuously pray? Give thanks always? Every part of me set apart for God—spirit, soul, and body? The God who called me is faithful to do what He promised?*

God spoke His Word to me, and while it was almost too good to be true, I was determined to believe it.

I then read the words of Jesus found in the four Gospels of Matthew, Mark, Luke, and John. I saw that while Jesus healed people from all their diseases during His ministry, He also touched their spiritual sickness. To many of those He healed He also said, "Your sins are forgiven." I realized then that my physical pain and spiritual sin were connected. Luke 10:9 especially spoke to me. When Jesus sent out His disciples, He told them, "Heal the sick who are there and tell them, 'The kingdom of God has come near to you.'"

I thought to myself, *Maybe the pain and struggles I am going through are because the Kingdom of God has come near me!* That gave me the hope I needed at that specific time. I kept imagining myself pushing past my pain through growing my faith.

I started to experience healing from my hardships and the emotional, mental, and personal problems I was having at that time. No matter the situation, I continued to find my strength in God's Word. I was encouraged next by the Apostle Paul's writings to Timothy where he wrote about his past, the things he had gone through, and how God had delivered him from all of it. Paul wrote, "For the Spirit God gave us does not make us timid, but gives us power, love and self-discipline. So do not be ashamed of the testimony about our Lord or of me his prisoner. Rather, join with me in suffering for the gospel, by the power of God. He has saved us and called us to a holy life—not because of anything we have done but because of his own purpose and grace." (2 Timothy 1:7-9)

Paul was reminding Timothy that, at that time, it seemed his way of life was just persecution, betrayal, and pain. As I read Paul's words, I wondered, *What is my purpose in life? My purpose for being?* I was questioning my faith. I was struggling with loving myself. I didn't know if I could endure like Paul did. Yet Paul's message reminded me that I had endured, and that God had already rescued me from all of it.

Then I came to 2 Timothy 3:10-12. Paul was again writing to Timothy. "You, however, know all about my teaching, my way of life, my purpose, faith, patience, love, endurance, persecutions, sufferings—what kinds of things happened to me in Antioch, Iconium and Lystra, the persecutions I endured. Yet the Lord rescued me from all of them. In fact, everyone who wants to live a godly life in Christ Jesus will be persecuted."

When I read that, it made me think, *Yes, I was in Saudi Arabia. Yes, I was in Yemen. Yes, I was in Northern Uganda. I was persecuted in all those places.*

Why?

Paul's words were teaching me that it was because I was trying to live a godly life in Jesus and proclaim the life that Christ had given me. Paul said he was rescued in all of them.

Then I began to think, *Maybe God will rescue me from the pain I am going through emotionally, mentally, and in every way.*

The New Testament passage that stood out the most was James 5:14-15. "Is anyone among you sick? Let them call the elders of the church to pray over them and anoint them with oil in the name of the Lord. And the prayer offered in faith will make the sick person well; the Lord will raise them up. If they have sinned, they will be forgiven." I wondered what it meant to "call the elders," and the Lord said, "You need to talk about your sickness with someone who can pray with you specifically."

I knew that would be a tough thing for me to do, but part of my healing first required back and forth conversations about my trauma with people I could confide in and trust, ministry partners and friends who provided oversight and accountability similar to what is provided by the elders of the church. Then, through prayer, I would be healed and restored.

Yet when I read, "If they have sinned, they will be forgiven," I was reminded how much bitterness, hate, and anger I had toward those who did wrong things to me.

I knew forgiveness would be hard. Did I want them to be forgiven by God? Part of me wanted them to go through what I went through.

Then James 5:16 concluded, "Therefore confess your sins to each other and pray for each other so that you may be healed. The prayer of a righteous person is powerful and effective."

Confess your sins to each other and pray for each other so that you may be healed? How could I possibly do that when I was preoccupied with evil wishes of my abusers being tortured while I watched—or even of me torturing them as I had been tortured?

Of me hacking the rapist to pieces with a machete before he could take another boy.

Of me firing the electrodes so the hot current could sear through my jailer's body.

Of me drilling the hole into the bone of my abuser before hanging him up to die.

The human side of me didn't want to confess and forgive. I wanted justice and revenge! I imagined seeing them murdered—and I felt *good* about it as I did.

I don't want to see these people. I don't want to be in a place where I confess, and then they confess their sins and pain to me.

I want them to die. All of them! Eye for an eye.

But Christ was teaching me that revenge was not mine to take. He taught forgiveness, even (and especially) when it was undeserved. In John 8, the Jewish teachers of the law and the Pharisees brought Jesus a woman caught in the act of adultery. They said to Christ, "'In the Law Moses commanded us to stone such women. Now what do you say?' They were using this question as a trap, in order to have a basis for accusing him. But Jesus bent down and started to write on the ground with his finger. When they kept on questioning him, he straightened up and said to them, 'Let any one of you who is without sin be the first to throw a stone at her.' Again he stooped down and wrote on the ground."

"At this, those who heard began to go away one at a time, the older ones first, until only Jesus was left, with the woman still standing there. Jesus straightened up and asked her, 'Woman, where are they? Has no one condemned you?' 'No one, sir,' she said. 'Then neither do I condemn you,' Jesus declared. 'Go now and leave your life of sin.'" (John 8:5-11)

Even more, Jesus taught that even having a sinful *thought* was the same as actually committing the sin (Matthew 5:21-30). Then I started thinking of how He said we are to love our enemies and pray for those who persecute us (Matthew 5:43-48).

I was filled with sinful thoughts about the sins done to me—but God needed me to also focus on my own sins. Yes, I hated them. I wanted to see them die, yet according to the scriptural principle, my hatred was *already* the same as murder. Even when we have been offended or abused, the Lord requires us to examine our own thoughts and identify the sins we are carrying that need to be confessed.

God was telling me that I had to take every moment of my emotional, mental, and physical pain and let it be the catalyst for forgiveness. He wanted me to realize that if I could someday go, meet with my abusers, and forgive them for their sins against me, it would be the beginning of a new chapter for my healing.

I struggled so much with letting others know my pain, but

ABDUCTED BUT NOT FORSAKEN

God wanted me to go back to the people who wronged me. I reluctantly prayed, "Lord, if that is your will, and that is what will bring healing, take me there."

If that was what it took, I had to do it. God wanted to use me to the uttermost parts of the world. But was it truly possible to go meet evil people and see the confession that brings healing? I remained unsure.

Finally, I looked at Revelation 21:4, which says, "He will wipe every tear from their eyes. There will be no more death or mourning or crying or pain, for the old order of things has passed away."

When I read "no more death," I couldn't help but feel like I was dying slowly inside.

I was mourning.

I was crying.

I was in pain.

That God would "wipe every tear from their eyes" was almost too much for my troubled soul to understand. I shed *lots* of tears when I was by myself. That was so hard to do, especially because I had been taught that a warrior does not cry, even when they are in pain, and especially not in front of other people. So, I could hold back my tears in public, but in private? I sobbed. My tears flowed. Just the idea that God could do what Revelation 21:4 claimed was beyond my understanding.

> I read and proclaimed God's Word to myself, even as I wrestled with doubt.

Still, I again allowed myself to be hopeful as I read and proclaimed God's Word to myself, even as I wrestled with doubt. I knew I would proclaim Him, and continue to do so, even when I didn't feel I had anyone to turn to or anywhere to go—and I thought once more, *The Kingdom of God has come! My healing can point to the Kingdom of God.*

I also tried to find out about others in modern times who had been through imprisonments and abuses similar to mine as a result of being a follower of Jesus. I discovered a group, still in operation today, that was created to empower those who were initiating the Jesus Movement within Islamic nations and communities around the world. I connected with them, and through their network I was able to use coded communications to interact with people living in Muslim countries. I was especially drawn to the missionaries in Morocco, whose experiences of persecution, depression, and anxiety weren't as extreme as what I had been through but were relatable.

That soon created an opportunity for me to go to Morocco, and I went to work on a plan to visit them.

I was still recovering. In many ways, I was still not healed emotionally, but I wanted to meet them.

I *needed* to.

I first went to Belfast, Northern Ireland for the next month. There, I made preparations for the trip before traveling to Morocco for a group conference where I met with one of the members who worked outside the capital city of Rabat. I found it to be a gorgeous city, located along the shores of the Bouregreg River and the Atlantic Ocean. Its mostly white buildings reflected the city's Islamic and French-colonial heritage. Its iconic Hassan Tower, a minaret dating to the twelfth century, soared above the ruins of a mosque.

Once again in a Muslim country, my emotions were up and down, both positive and negative. Yet I recognized that the level of the people's commitment to their Islamic faith was different. I could tell some of them were not extreme. There was more of a European influence. Therefore, it was unlike what I'd seen in Saudi Arabia, Yemen, and some other countries I'd been to before. It was another new learning experience, and I felt that God's call to use me to the uttermost parts of the world was being renewed in my heart. I was convinced the Lord had brought me to Morocco.

In no time, I resumed what I had been doing before in obedience to God's calling: building new relationships and sharing my story and the love of God in hopes of establishing new followers of Jesus.

My approach was the same, too. I was open and direct with nothing hidden.

But that quickly became a problem for the group. While I wasn't controlled by them, the way I went about sharing my story was not the way they operated. They worked different jobs in those countries. Once they formed relationships with Muslim individuals through that work, only then would they share about God, and it was done privately and quietly.

There is wisdom to that approach—but that was not me.

I knew I could be arrested and imprisoned again, but I didn't care about what I had gone through in the past that got me into trouble. The moment people were in front of me, it was a chance to love on them, tell my story, and hear their stories.

I did not hold back. Anyone who has been around me for any length of time has likely heard me say, "If you are doing something that you don't want others to know about, then you should not be doing it in the first place." I took every opportunity I had to declare Him who had given me life and delivered me from what could have consumed me to death.

I simply could not hide it!

The Bible, the gospel of Jesus Christ, is to be heard as well as seen. It is proclaimed in words, but it is also demonstrated and attested to by signs and wonders. Acts 8:5-8 tells us about Philip. "Philip went down to a city in Samaria and proclaimed the Messiah there. When the crowds heard Philip and saw the signs he performed, they all paid close attention to what he said. For with shrieks, impure spirits came out of many, and many who were paralyzed or lame were healed. So there was great joy in that city."

At that point, I felt that *I* was a demonstration of God's signs and wonders. Only He had kept me alive all of those times when I could have died. Part of God's call to me was that I would go through challenges—and I would not have survived them without His miraculous power in my life. I believe healing and joy will come and deliverance will occur whenever Jesus is proclaimed with courage and preached in truth and power.

So, I began praying for people in Morocco, entering into spiritual warfare through those prayers. I knew that when I had done this in other places, I had sometimes encountered demonic manifestations.

I went to the marketplace in Rabat and was talking about my story, including my past imprisonments, the treatment I'd received, and how God was healing me from those experiences. As people asked questions about me, I also talked about my medical work and declared how God had brought me to where I was at that moment. A man named Ikra came up to me, spoke to me for a few moments, and then introduced me to Ibrahim—an adherent to non-denominational Islam (a faction different from the Sunni, Shia, and other Islam sects I had encountered) who had a role in the leadership counsel in Rabat.

As I talked to Ibrahim, I decided I wanted him to introduce me to some of the other Muslim leaders there known as "men of peace."

Ibrahim said he could do that, but he needed to learn more about who I was and why I was in Morocco so that he could introduce me and my mission in Rabat appropriately to those leaders. "I could come with you to your house and tell you more," I said.

Ibrahim seemed hesitant. I added, "I have a good gift that I want to share with you when we get to your home." As I said this to him, I wasn't thinking that I could possibly encounter demons at his home. I knew nothing about Ibrahim other than his role in the leadership council and that he was one of the "men of peace."

His eyes widened. "Oh, yeah? You have a gift for me?" He was cheerful as we began to journey to his house, and his curiosity got the best of him "What kind of gift is it?" he asked. He could see that I didn't have a big bag with me that could hold a gift.

"I will show you the gift when we get there," I assured him.

When we arrived, Ibrahim introduced me to his family, but then his entire demeanor changed. He went from happy to sullen, frustrated, and borderline angry. He began apologizing as others gathered around. He kept saying, "Things are not good here. I'm sorry."

With those words, fear surged through me. *Am I about to be beaten or tortured?* I did everything to hide how afraid I was, but inside I was shaken to the core. I recalled the many captors who would say to me, "I am so sorry. I apologize for what I am about to do. It is my job."

His words were a trigger, and I didn't know what was happening. I tried to keep myself together. "It's okay," I insisted. "I don't understand why you are apologizing. What's going on?"

He paused and looked right at me. Then his gaze softened. "One of my sons has been sick. He hasn't gotten out of bed in over five months. I am embarrassed to bring guests here."

He sat down, suddenly looking exhausted. "I chose to bring you here because you said you were *tabib* (a "doctor" or "healer" in Arabic), and I thought you might be able to give me some advice. Also, you said you had a gift. I thought maybe you knew about my son's situation." It was then that I realized Ibrahim must've assumed Ikra had told me about his sick son when he had not.

I asked him where his son was, and Ibrahim took me into

the back room. Even then, I couldn't help but think I was a sheep being led to the slaughter. Once we were there, though, it was exactly as he had said. His son was there, lying on the floor, and his mother and some of the other women were there as well. It was clear the son was completely helpless. One of his wives welcomed me. *"Ahlaan bik Doktor."* she said.

I thanked her in response. *"Afwan"* She smiled, probably because I was a foreigner who could speak her language. That began to set me at ease.

I knew I was safe—and that infused my confidence and trust in the Lord.

"I know someone who has conquered sickness," I said. "He gives life and maintains life. He heals. We can trust the Lord."

As I spoke encouragement and hope in the Lord, the son kept muttering something I couldn't make out and began looking straight into my eyes. I didn't know exactly what he was doing. He stretched like he was trying to reach out to me, and his mother tried to push his hand down.

I was filled with compassion for this young man and his family. "Would you be okay if I prayed for your son right now?" I asked.

The moment prayer is mentioned to Muslims, they will not say "no." I received permission, and then I went to the son, knelt down, and placed my hands on him. I could tell Ibrahim and the others didn't want me to do that because the son was in such poor condition, but I did it—and I prayed in the name of Jesus.

"You are the one who heals!" I declared aloud.

When I finished the prayer, the son got up, started speaking, and then began yelling, *"Isa ibn Maryam! Isa ibn Maryam!"*

He was shouting, "Jesus, the son of Mary! Jesus, the son of Mary!"

His yelling caused a commotion both inside and outside Ibrahim's home. The son instantly became violent, and even as some of the family tried to pin him down, I could see the awe they felt, wondering how the son, who hadn't risen out of bed for months, was now acting the way he was.

I helped to hold him still and then heard a voice in my mind tell me, "Start casting out the demons."

I began praying louder and louder, commanding the demons to leave him. Suddenly, the son settled down and sat while still being held, but he was no longer violent. I kept praying, and he vomited. Some of the substance sprayed on my legs, but I did not care. I wanted the oppressed to be set free!

The son started to shout with a sober, firm voice. *"Ana Shafiat! Ana Shafiat! Ana Shafiat! Ana Shafiat!"* He was declaring, "I am healed! I am healed! I am healed! I am healed!"

Joy spread throughout the home, and most everyone looked at me, which made me uncomfortable. I had cast out demons before, but never in the house of a Muslim leader like Ibrahim—but God did it! I was just the messenger. Not only was I trembling as a result of the experience, but I also felt as though energy had left me.

As things began to settle, some asked me, "Who are you?" "Where are you from?" "Why are you doing miracles? That's God's doing, glory to Him Most High!"

I was completely taken aback by what had just happened. It had nothing to do with me. It was a miracle of God in the power of Jesus' name!

In that confrontation with the devil in Morocco, the demon was cast out of Ibrahim's son. He even started to speak, saying, *"Isa al-Masih! Isa al-Masih!"* Earlier, he was saying, "Jesus, the son of Mary," which is something all Muslims know. But when he proclaimed *Isa al-Masih*—"Jesus the Messiah"—I knew in my spirit that the demons had left him, and he believed in Jesus the Messiah.

As those in and around the house heard him, they responded,

"Allahu Akbar! Allahu Akbar!" That meant, "God is the greatest! God is the greatest!"

Ibrahim's son was healed and restored, and God was glorified!

In no time, the news spread, and as it did, it drew unexpected attention to me, causing some of the missionaries in the group to distance themselves from me. In the meantime, I spent the next three days with Ibrahim's family. During that time, I discipled them the way that Jesus modeled in the Bible. I shared with them Bible stories they knew as Muslims, such as the account of the Good Samaritan, followed by a question-and-answer period where we discussed

Ibrahim's son was healed and restored, and God was glorified!

and had dialogue about the stories. While it was exhausting for me, the family was not tired because of the energy that was present after what had happened to the son.

Ibrahim also confided to me that they had taken his son to five different places that practiced what I categorized as witchcraft, and that each one had done rituals in an attempt to heal him. Even though his son was physically sick, Ibrahim and his family didn't realize he was possessed by demonic spirits until they were cast out. They were mesmerized that someone like me, who knew nothing about such rituals, could succeed where everything else had failed.

I again told them that it wasn't me, but God, who had delivered the son from demons and physically healed him. That made a huge impact on Ibrahim and his family. Incredibly, Ibrahim confessed Christ as Savior during my time with them, as did some of his family members privately in their hearts.

My intention was to stay longer with Ibrahim's family, but on the third day, after the evening prayer was proclaimed, I was picked up by the state security police and taken to a place where I could be questioned. They had heard what had happened with Ibrahim's son, and they asked the usual questions I'd heard so often before during an interrogation: "Who are you?" "Where did you come from?" "Why are you here?"

Since I knew I was already in trouble, I answered, "I came to proclaim Jesus Christ and Him who rose from the dead. Jesus forgives our sins when we confess, He still heals, and by His stripes we were healed. He has done all that to me personally, and I can witness to that. I am one of His followers, and He sent me here as His disciple. Okongo is my name. I came from the United Kingdom, but I was actually born in Kenya."

Because I live for Christ, that was my identity. That was where I came from. I was His product. I responded in a way I thought would give glory to Him alone.

As they left the interrogation room, I didn't know when they were coming back or what was going on, and I started wondering what was going to happen next. When I had been interrogated in the past, I'd never been left alone. Someone was always kept behind to keep an eye on me. My thoughts were all over the place until, a while later, two of them returned.

One accused, "Who told you that you can come here and cause public disorder?"

"Sir, I did not come to cause public disorder," I pleaded. "If you are referring to what happened to the young man, then it's the doing of God, our healer and Savior. That can only be done by God alone. No human can do such a thing. Even though I was involved, I did not determine the outcome and the man's freedom. But, if this is a case of 'who,' then I know it's God who caused his healing to be publicized. I am sorry that this is considered a public disorder in your books."

I was actually surprised they allowed me to give such a long explanation without interrupting me. That had certainly not been my experience with previous police interrogations, but I thought I gave a sincere and truthful explanation that would hopefully get me out of trouble since I had already been tagged with the crime of public disorder.

I'm convinced God wants us to stand up and be counted by speaking the truth. When I was asked who I was, I didn't go on the defensive and say, "I like Mohammed and Allah." I had done that before in Saudi Arabia, and I was determined never to lie about, or deny, my relationship with Christ ever again.

Instead, I said I was there because of Jesus. It wasn't boasting. I knew the potential consequences of my words. But Christ told us not to fear, panic, or retreat because He would empower us to speak those things that bring glory to Him.

I was put in prison, and my treatment while incarcerated in Rabat was not at all as bad as it was in Al-Ha'ir. I was held in three different places over a three-week period. When I told the officials in Morocco that I would be willing to leave the country and never come back, I received only three lashes on my backside and was released. Compared to what I had endured at Saudi Arabia, Yemen, or Sudan, that was a slap on the wrist. Later, I learned that Ibrahim had used his influence and position as one of the leaders in Rabat to help secure my release from prison.

Today, I am still friends with four of Ibrahim's many sons as well as some of his wives and other family members. Those who have made mission trips with me to Morocco and met Ibrahim before he died in 2011 will tell you how the deep, pure love he had for me always brought me to tears. It was not unusual for him to get down on his knee like he was worshipping, and then I'd go over, we would hug, and he would kiss my neck.

The son who was delivered and healed by God has also passed away. He died a few years before his father did, but he was still a follower of God, though he experienced persecution as a result of his belief in Jesus. Others in Ibrahim's family have not publicly professed Christ, which is understandable. There are so many Muslims who I strongly believe are followers of Jesus, and they have not formally made it public knowledge because they don't want to be persecuted. Ibrahim's family always gives me a warm reception each time I visit and talk to them, and I am glad they are a part of the outreach ministry in Morocco and a partner with Unite 4 Africa.

When God starts to work on our hearts, we become one, and we embrace each other because of how God has worked in our lives. For example, it is not the cultural norm in Muslim communities to shake hands or hug other men, but in Ibrahim's home, where I am considered family, they will shake my hand and hug me.

It's one of the ways God has marked my life and my ministry. People join with me in a new and different way as God shows His love to us.

In 1 Corinthians 9:22-23, Paul said, "I have become all things to all people so that by all possible means I might save some. I do all this for the sake of the gospel, that I may share in its blessings." This is what I try to do when I minister in Muslim countries. I also try to model my activities after what Jesus did in John 4 when He met with the woman at the well. According to the culture at that time, Christ was not supposed to be in contact with a Samaritan woman, much less engage in conversation with her. Yet He not only spoke to her, he related to her personally and culturally. He declared truth to her—and, when she discovered He was the Messiah and believed in Him, she told others, and "many of the Samaritans from that town believed in him because of the woman's testimony." (John 4:39)

That is as much my passion today as it was then, and I couldn't wait to see what God was going to do next after my time in Morocco.

Chapter 5

RENEWED CALLING, RENEWED ABUSE

I got on a plane to Spain and then to Belfast. I wanted to recover and ponder my next move—and consider how to follow up with Ibrahim about the other "men of peace" like him that he had told me about and that I could visit elsewhere.

While in Belfast, I learned about a different group that was trying to help people dealing with mental issues, and I decided to become a part of it. It provided a chance for me to again use my medical training to study how mental and emotional issues affected people's lives. It also allowed me to tap into their knowledge and try to apply it to my own mental and emotional issues.

I didn't want to fully share my past experiences with them, though. It was still hard for me to open up to people.

Through that group, I learned about a missionary working in Mauritania who had been through a lot of trauma, some of it the result of persecution. As I found out more about his experiences, I became more passionate to go there. I thought that I could go to that West African nation and do things differently than he did and perhaps be more effective in sharing my story and God's love. I also thought I could go there and use my medical expertise to help others, especially in the schools.

Yet as I became more convinced that God was leading me to go to Mauritania, others from the different groups I had been working with started telling me that I should consider taking a break for a season of healing. So, I mostly stayed put in Northern Ireland for the next six months and used the time to rest while also solidifying my friendship with the friends I had there. I did get away to Kenya for a couple of weeks, too, spending time with my two brothers: Jack, who was a chaplain, and David, who was a pediatrician. Both served those roles at Kijabe Mission Hospital where I had previously done medical research with Dr. Ace Barnes. He was a pathologist and friend who usually went to Kijabe once or twice each year, and he was there when I visited. All three men were incredible supporters of the work I was doing, and it was good to go home for a brief stay.

One of my friends in Northern Ireland was Dr. John McIlvenna, who accompanied me to Kenya when he was a medical student. I spoke in his church a few times. He introduced me to Donald McConnell, a farmer who had a large farm with sheep and other livestock and became one of my supporters while I was in Northern Ireland. I also became friends with Belfast pastor John O'Neill. We sang songs together such as "Jesus, All for Jesus" by Robin Mark, a Christian singer, songwriter, worship leader, and recording artist based in Belfast. His song "Days of Elijah" has been sung in churches the world over since he published it in 1996. Just being able to use Robin's music to tell Jesus that He is all I am and ever hope to be, and that I surrender all my ambitions, hopes, and plans into His hands, encouraged me greatly and still moves me to tears today.

These individuals and many others became sources of healing for me during those six months.

On a few occasions, I volunteered to work on Donald's farm. I'll never forget the day he allowed me to go for a ride on the plane that dusted his fields with insecticide. I'd never seen crop dusting before, much less rode on the airplane as it circled, dived, and flew low just above the lush, hilly, green rows of vegetation. I felt as excited as Curious George as I experienced how the spraying was done—but I was even more surprised when, during the flight, the Lord spoke to me.

"Okongo, I want to send you to the uttermost parts of the world to spray the message of the gospel to others, just like you see the spreading of the chemicals to take care of and heal the plants. I need you to go."

There it was, His calling, and I responded just like I did back when I was 16 years old in Kenya.

I want to go.

God affirmed, "I want to use you to go to the places where no one wants to go."

I realized, *Yes, Lord. The harvest is plenty. It's not about the spraying. It's about the harvest it will produce. The harvest I will see as I declare you!*

With that added revelation, I became more determined than ever to go to Mauritania, and my conversations by phone with Ibrahim allowed me to make new contacts with prominent "men of peace" in Afghanistan, Iran, Iraq, Pakistan, Libya, Algeria, Egypt, Somalia, Syria, Chad, Niger, Jordan, and, yes, Yemen and Saudi Arabia. He also introduced me to people in India, Tunisia, and Lebanon, some of whom traveled to meet with me in the United Kingdom. In addition, Ibrahim connected me with a business partner in the United Arab Emirates.

My contacts and influences started to expand, all in dramatic confirmation of God's words to me in the plane over Donald's farm. It was all falling into place with God's vision, and much of that was the direct result of what had happened in Morocco. This increased my healing, as well as brought affirmation instead of rejection since there were still other Christians who were afraid to be associated with me because of the imprisonments and torture that had happened to me previously.

I had to go — trusting God as He led me step by step.

The Lord did not reveal exactly how everything was going to unfold. I didn't know how any of it was going to be accommodated or funded. Would it happen through other agencies within those countries? Who would host me on these journeys? Would I be safe, or could I be arrested and persecuted again? Was I going to experience more supernatural miracles like I'd seen with Ibrahim's son?

I did not know any of the answers.

All I knew was that I had to go—trusting God as He led me step by step.

At the close of the six months in Northern Ireland, I went from Belfast, first to London and then to Dakar, Senegal to visit with friends there for two days, before heading north to Mauritania. I journeyed to the capital city, Nouakchott, which, like Dakar, is located right on the West African coast. Mauritania is a mostly desert country with a turbulent history. It has seen many different government and military coups since it became independent from France in 1960. Today, it is officially called the Islamic Republic of Mauritania, and it was a Sunni Muslim country when I visited.

Before I arrived, I knew about the restrictions and suffering there. Mauritania had been criticized for its poor human rights record, including its poverty and continued practice of slavery (from bonded labor to domestic child brides and human trafficking)—but I was excited to meet the Islamic preacher Ibrahim had recommended as a "man of peace" and hoped to establish a base with him.

I ended up visiting with him for an entire week while staying in a hotel. I was received, and because Ibrahim was a Muslim, I was seen as someone prominent, almost like a V.I.P. Daily, I received food from them as a form of payment for being there: roast lamb, fish balls, rice with vegetables. It was delicious. But, while there was no overt animosity shown toward me, the preacher and the others with him became more skeptical of me with each day. They remained inquisitive as I talked about who I was and what I did in Morocco, but they were not as receptive as I'd hoped.

Meanwhile, when I was in the city near my hotel, I was shocked at the depth of impoverishment among the people. I was careful when I went out. I understood that any guest in Mauritania was closely monitored, though I don't believe the security agents at that time were government sponsored. I did know it was one of the top countries for kidnapping of foreigners, particularly Westerners. Still, I couldn't help but visit with the people in the streets to hear their stories, what little they told me. Most of them did not feel free to open up to me because they knew speaking with a foreigner placed them at risk.

As I continued meeting with Ibrahim's friend, the Islamic preacher, I began to realize that he was a more radical Muslim than I originally thought. I remained upfront with him about who I was and what I was doing, yet the more I spoke about Christ, the more I thought I was perceived by him as a threat. The language barrier between us was also a challenge. It was close to Arabic, but not quite as precise, so clear communication was not always easy.

I'll always remember when I joined them for a function near the city and saw slavery for myself. It's truly impossible to fully understand, or even articulate, such horrific oppression until you actually see it. I did, and it moved me deeply. Therefore, when we returned, I declared to my host, the Islamic preacher, that what I'd seen was wrong, inhuman, and anti-god—and I was so distraught from what I had seen, I wasn't even able to eat what I was offered at a dinner reception they held that night. I thought it was disgraceful to be offered an expensive meal after the suffering I had witnessed. I felt like Moses who, after growing up as the son of Pharaoh's daughter, chose to be mistreated among the people of God rather than enjoy the fleeting pleasures of sin (Hebrews 11:24-25). I wanted to stand up and be counted for those who were oppressed.

From that moment on, my relationship with the preacher and his friends began to break apart. I started to transition myself away from time with Ibrahim's friend to visit others I knew who lived outside of Nouakchott, expatriates who I had also been introduced to when I was in Northern Ireland. Some of them were from Nigeria, and I visited them twice to see how they were doing with a school they were operating in the area.

Then, 10 days into my stay in Mauritania, I was visited by three men. They were very friendly, and they asked me all kinds of questions about many things, including my faith. I suspected they were security spies, but I shared my opinions about slavery as well as my feelings against the marginalization I'd observed between white and black Mauritanians.

The trio were with the police, and I was arrested.

The accusation: blasphemy against Islam.

I was blindfolded, something that had never happened to me before, not even when I was in the camp of the Lord's Resistance Army all those years earlier. It frightened me, and it kept me from knowing where I was taken to be interrogated. They questioned me, wanting to know if I was an activist who intended to start a movement with the people. That was something the authorities would view as a terrorist act. At first, I defended myself, insisting that I was not a terrorist or in the country to cause some sort of uprising. But then I doubled down.

"What you guys are doing," I told them, "is evil, sinful, and needs to be exposed." I was direct and blunt, and my candor had its predictable consequences.

For the next seven days, I was incarcerated and beaten. I was slapped and thrown around. My head was pounded into the wall or smashed into the ground. I was whacked on the bottoms of my feet by a baton. Most of the time, I was in handcuffs, even when I was provided food, and I was sometimes given different clothes and moved—all to be tortured again, and all while wearing the blindfold.

It was terrible.

Once I was in the same room with another prisoner who began a conversation with me. He asked about my accent. "Are you French? Or perhaps Nigerian British?" he questioned.

"Maybe," I replied. I was nervous to talk with him because, with my blindfold, I could not see who he was, and I thought he might be someone sent to interrogate and pump information from me. I didn't know who I could trust. "I am just a servant of the living God," I said, "and I came here to do God's work."

However, after our captors came in and beat him, I realized he was indeed a prisoner like me. I felt safe to talk further with him, and he told me he was a native of Mauritania and had been imprisoned himself because he was standing up for his people against the corrupt, evil government. He went on to speak about human trafficking, the killing of people if they opposed the government, and the religious oppression they faced. Shortly after that, we were separated, and I never got to talk with him again.

My captors were brutally efficient at what they did. I'll never forget, on the sixth day of my imprisonment during a brief time I was not blindfolded, they brought in a helmet that looked just like the type someone would wear when riding a motorbike. I thought perhaps they wanted me to put it on to protect me from any further injuries to my head.

My relief immediately turned to horror when they slipped it on, and I felt the volts hit my scalp.

It was an electrified helmet.

Mercifully, I was freed the next day. I was allowed to wash, and for the first time I was able to eat without having my hands bound. When I was released, I was immediately taken to the airport, my passport was returned along with the few belongings I had brought with me, and I was placed on a plane to Senegal. When we landed, I was allowed to use the phone in security, and I contacted my friends there. They looked after me in Dakar for the next week, which included a trip to the hospital to receive treatment for my wounds.

I also began studying again about how Christ's disciples handled persecution. I read about how the Apostle John was boiled in oil before being sent into exile on the island of Patmos, the place where he wrote what we now know as the book of Revelation. I looked at James, who was killed with the sword on the order of King Herod and was the first of the disciples to become a martyr because of his faith in Christ. Peter, Andrew, and Philip were all crucified. Thomas was thrust through with a spear, and Matthew was fatally stabbed. Other disciples were later killed by hanging or stoning.

Who am I? I thought. *I haven't had to experience all those things. Yet those who walked with Jesus so passionately served the Lord faithfully, even to the point of death.*

I came to the conclusion that I had to continue on because I hadn't come close to that level of suffering. I recalled Paul's words in Philippians 1:21 where he wrote, "For to me, to live is Christ and to die is gain."

I will not stop going, I decided anew, *no matter what.*

When I arrived back in Northern Ireland, I kept to myself and felt a renewed sense of grief and shame because of my trauma. Several people had told me not to go to Mauritania, just as they had insisted that I shouldn't go to Morocco. "You need to heal," they pleaded. "Don't get involved. That's not the right thing to do." They were also worried I could be abducted in Mauritania.

But I'd gone anyway and was once more incarcerated and abused.

Was this you, God? I wondered. *Why me?*

I questioned myself more than ever, and while I tried to heal, I did not open up about how I was feeling to anyone. I was deeply troubled—yet God continued telling me, "I will use you."

I began thinking about the glimmer of hope I'd seen in the eyes of the street children in Mauritania. I remembered the poverty and slavery I had witnessed and recalled that I'd been bold enough to speak out against it. Suddenly, it wasn't the pain I'd experienced in prison that mattered to me, but the pain of the people. It was clear God wanted to do so many things through me, and I kept hearing Him say, "You need to give yourself so you can be used because if you don't, who will?"

Even as I struggled with doubt, a burden built within me. *Many people are still suffering. How will they be delivered? How will they be saved? How will they be restored?*

My passion for the lost and hurting rang loud and true within me! Seeing the suffering of others, and experiencing my own suffering, inspired me to not be quiet and to think beyond myself and my needs. I could hear the voice of God declare, "It will take people who are willing to sacrifice to make a difference!"

My passion for the lost and hurting rang loud and true within me!

The Lord also confirmed Himself to me through the financial support I received from others, including Ibrahim and his networks of contacts, to do what I was doing.

When I thought of Ibrahim, a part of me resented him because of how the Islamic preacher in Mauritania did not turn out to be a "man of peace" at all, but a radical. Yet a bigger part of me saw what God had miraculously done, and was still doing, for Ibrahim and his family. At the time, Ibrahim was reading the Bible in chronological order and often emailed me questions about what he was reading as he went. I had encouraged him to start in the Old Testament with Genesis and the New Testament with the book of John. I thought that was the best approach to help him understand the Bible as a whole.

Not long after my return from Mauritania, I received an email from Ibrahim. He knew I had traveled to Mauritania but did not know I had returned or what had happened while I was there. He wrote, "This is your gift. Deuteronomy 31:6. Be strong and courageous. Do not be afraid or terrified because of them, for the Lord your God goes with you. He will never leave you nor forsake you." Then he added, "There is no one who can explain this experience better than you."

I cannot describe how it felt to read that. It brought me to tears. After one suffers as I had, messages like that are like a touch of heaven.

I didn't reply at first. I was still trying to recover from what had happened in Mauritania. A few days later, before I could respond, Ibrahim emailed again. "I have another gift for you," it said. "Blessed is the one who perseveres under trial because, having stood the test, that person will receive the crown of life that the Lord has promised to those who love him." I knew that was from James 1:12.

A few hours later, another email came from my friend. "Cast all your anxiety on him because he cares for you." That was from 1 Peter 5:7.

Where is he getting all of this? I thought. *After all, he's a new convert.*

I decided that I needed to talk to Ibrahim rather than write him via email. In the meantime, he sent yet another message.

From 2 Corinthians 4:17, it said that our present troubles are small, yet they produce a glory that vastly outweighs them and will last forever. Then he wrote again. It was the words of Jesus from John 14:1. "Do not let your hearts be troubled. You believe in God; believe also in me."

Amazed, I set up a time to speak with him that Saturday. On Friday night, Ibrahim sent the words of John 16:33. "I have told you these things, so that in me you may have peace. In this world you will have trouble. But take heart! I have overcome the world."

When I was on the phone with him, I couldn't wait.

"Why are you writing these things to me," I asked incredulously. "Where are they coming from?" My attitude was that Ibrahim had just become a believer in Jesus. I knew God. I knew the Scriptures. Who was he to share these things with me? Sadly, I belittled him in my mind.

"I really don't know," he said, and I could hear the joy in his voice. "Each time I open the book, I read them, and I am told to write them to you. I don't know what is going on. I am just doing what I feel I need to do."

"Who is telling you?" I pressed.

"I don't know. I just feel a need to do it."

It was hard for me to believe and accept that a recently converted follower of Christ could send such messages that healed me to my very core. "I still believe God called you," he told me. "Some will not accept what God is doing, but I've been a part of what you do, and it has changed my life!"

For the next six hours, we talked and cried. I shared a few more details about my time in Mauritania, but I kept things vague enough so as not to cause Ibrahim to feel guilt and shame for connecting me with his friend, the Islamic preacher. I also didn't want to share any details about my bad experiences there.

"I don't know what this is," Ibrahim said, "but I hear a voice speaking something in me. What we suffer now is nothing compared to the glory he will reveal to us."

"Ibrahim, do you know that's the Bible?" I asked.

"I don't know what it is."

"It's Romans 8:18," I replied.

Ibrahim was a Muslim who had just been converted, but his encouragement brought fresh hope and healing into my life. I felt like he was not only accepting me, but he was accepting what the Lord was doing in his life. I had no right to belittle my friend. I needed to repent of my pride and unbelief.

God spoke to me through Ibrahim—and that gave me more passion to say to myself, "I *will* go to all these other places!" It was humbling, and it reenergized my servant's heart.

When I was in prison in Mauritania, I thought it could be the end of me. I'd never been blindfolded before. I was tortured yet again.

Now I was ready once more to *go*.

Go wherever God led and sacrifice in whatever way He required.

That opportunity came next through an organization called Tearfund, a Christian international relief organization that's still active today. I had heard about them previously when I was in southern Sudan, but I was formally introduced to Tearfund by the mayor of Belfast and some other friends in Northern Ireland who thought I might be a good fit with the charity. Since it focused on relief and development for disadvantaged communities and those in poverty, its mission was different from the one God had given me—but I saw an opportunity through Tearfund to get into some of the countries where Ibrahim had identified other "men of peace" for me to meet.

I met in Belfast with Tearfund organizational leaders, and we agreed that instead of being on their staff, I could serve them best as a consultant by observing and evaluating what they were doing in other countries. We signed a deal for four months, and with Tearfund's help in securing travel visas, I was able to go to numerous places: Yemen, Afghanistan, Uganda, Syria, Pakistan, Nepal, Lebanon, Jordan, and Iraq. I was also able to return to Ethiopia and southern Sudan, places I had previously visited. I used funding from my own supporters to cover the expenses, but I traveled as a representative of Tearfund. In each country, I either phoned or personally met with the "men of peace" Ibrahim had identified, promising to return to them independently in the future.

As my time with Tearfund came to an end, I met some people from the east African country of Eritrea who visited me in Belfast. They were exiles, but they shared with me the love they had for their people. That led me to decide to go there next, and after I arrived in Asmara, the capital city of Eritrea, I began having gatherings of Christian believers in their homes. I also met with missionaries there who were Eritrean Orthodox. From them, I learned of the oppression that existed in Eritrea, particularly regarding religion. Any religious group that wished to be legally recognized had to register with the Eritrean government. Most of those were either Islam or Eritrean Orthodox. The missionaries also showed me a school and a clinic they operated, and I was happy to help them in any way I could.

There was a conflict, though, between their Orthodox beliefs and traditions and the way I understood and presented Scripture. The two were totally different, and with each day, the missionaries wanted me to conform more with their Orthodox teachings and ways. Specifically, they felt I was more Protestant and Pentecostal than I should be. Christians who were deemed to be non-traditional usually faced severe persecution from both the Eritrean government and the Eritrean Orthodox Church. I saw firsthand how Christian converts from Muslim backgrounds, and cross denominational converts from Orthodox backgrounds, were harshly mistreated by their families and communities. It saddened me deeply.

This ultimately led to another confrontation with governmental authorities. "All religious groups must be registered in Eritrea. You need to be registered," they said.

"I don't need to be registered," I countered. "Yes, I am Pentecostal. Yes, I am Protestant. I am all these because I am a believer, a follower of Christ."

"Are you an orthodox?" they challenged.

"I'm not an orthodox," I said. "I'm a follower of Jesus. I'm here doing what He called me to do everywhere I go. I came here to meet and serve the people of Eritrea, to see what God is doing through the Orthodox church here, and to see if I can be of any help to them."

I was found guilty of promoting Pentecostalism and having house-to-house gatherings of Christian believers without legal registration to do so. I was then transported away from Asmara to a prison. I didn't know exactly where I was, but there were many prisoners there. As I was interrogated, punished, and whipped, I was regretful and thought, *Maybe I should've lied and said I was an orthodox so I wouldn't get into trouble. That is all I would have had to do.*

Unlike other prisons I'd been in previously, this one was more open. The inmates could walk about freely and talk with each other—but I was hesitant. I did not want to share anything about my story with them. I was frustrated, confused, and hurting, becoming more worried, doubtful, and angry toward God for allowing me to again be in this situation.

I remained that way until the fourth night of my incarceration. That was when I heard God speak to me.

"Why are you here?"

"I came to Eretria for the mission you called me to do, and to create opportunities to share the gospel," I quietly muttered. "Now I am where I shouldn't be, where I can't do anything, and where I can't serve people."

"Where are you?" God's voice prompted.

"Clearly, I'm in prison," I grumbled angrily.

"Who is with you?"

That's when my eyes were opened. I realized that I was with the exact people God wanted me to minister to. I had been in prison before. I knew what it was like, and here I was again—but with the opportunity to interact with the other prisoners directly.

That next morning, I began telling my story to anyone who would listen. I did that so often over the next three days that some of the inmates started calling me "imam." I began passionately singing as well, to the point where some inmates sang along with me, even though they didn't understand the words or their meaning. They were compelled to join in with me as I sang the lyrics to "God Will Make A Way" by Don Moen. I declared how the Lord worked in ways we cannot see, how He holds us closely to His side, and how He gives us love and strength for each new day. It was such a profound experience for me.

> I realized that I was with the exact people God wanted me to minister to.

By the end of my seventh day of incarceration, some told me they wanted to surrender their lives to Christ and follow the teaching and Bible stories I was giving to them.

I was so encouraged. *Wow! This must be God! He brought me here for a good reason, so I might as well keep doing what I'm doing, unless they decide to kill me.*

On the evening of the eighth day, I began praying over the

prisoners during the several hours each day or night when we were left alone by our captors. As I did, they started praying loud, then louder still. It was positively Pentecostal in nature, the very thing I was accused of being.

It was a powerful move of God—but it was one that got all of us into more trouble. We were all brought together and whipped, and the following morning when the event was further investigated by the authorities, I was pointed out as the one who instigated it and who brought "this evil spirit" into the prison.

Instantly, I was taken from the facility and transported to a large shipping container somewhere in the middle of the desert. I was forced inside, and I found myself crammed in there with many other people. It was outdoors, and even though the top of the tall, smooth container was open, there was no place to move.

We stood side-by-side, many of us tied together, all day and all night. Daytime temperatures inside the container were scorching hot. At night, it was bone-chillingly cold.

It was miserable—but I remembered what God had told me days earlier.

I told my story to those next to me.

I declared the love of Jesus.

Many of the prisoners with me were Muslim, and some died those two days and nights. As they took their final breaths, many said, "I hear God and the Jesus you are talking about. They're calling me, telling me that eternal life is through Him. I accept Jesus now as my Savior, and I am going to eternity right now. Thank you so much for telling me the gospel."

Witnessing their last-minute confessions to eternity was one of the most profound moments of my entire life.

When I was removed from the container and returned to the prison, I could not sleep. There was joy coming from the reality of God and His Son, but also the sadness of seeing someone die right next to me. As the two emotions collided, I was amazed that God could work in a situation where I did not even think, see, or imagine He could. It made me that much more determined. *I am willing to do whatever it takes to see one more soul come to the Lord!*

I also concluded that this was going to be the time I was going to die, and I wanted to die like those I'd seen in that container.

Twice more, I prayed and sang with the inmates in the prison, saw God move in a loud, dramatic fashion—and twice more I was taken to the container where I told others of God's love and watched them die after they accepted Him as Lord. I convinced myself, *This is how God is going to take me home with Him.*

It was not easy to see people die at my side, or to endure the emotion and pain, knowing I might be next, but I found hope and strength in it.

I determined that I was not going to stop—even if it meant my own death.

Finally, and quite unexpectedly, I was set free. The prison officials decided that I was not Pentecostal after all, but they also couldn't understand the "evil spirit" I was bringing into their facility, and they didn't want to. So, they got rid of me by allowing me to leave Eritrea.

I often think it would be better if God just told me in advance what would happen to me, but the Lord does things the way He does to remind me that His ways are not my ways, and His will is not my will.

With that perspective in mind, I could only wonder where He was going to take me next.

Here I am with three of my 15 siblings, Kenya. I'm much happier than I look here.

Five of us with my father, Jeck, in Kenya.

As a teenager,
after my abduction by the LRA.

With my father after the LRA abduction.
A couple of well-dressed gentlemen.

My mother, Judith, and my father, Jeck,
with me in Kandaria, Kenya.

With my brothers Jack,
David, Jacob, and Sylas
in Kenya in 1992.

The entire family in Kenya: (Top, left to right) Jeck, Judith, Jack, Dorothy, David, Pamela, Rose, Me , Annah, Jeniffer, and Sylas. (Bottom, left to right) Tim, John, Ruth, and Susan. Three of my siblings are not pictured here because they had passed away.

At a DIGUNA outreach in Africa.

With my high school friends in Kenya. Who needs shirts, right?

A crusade gathering in Africa where I told my story.

With members of the Sudan Army.

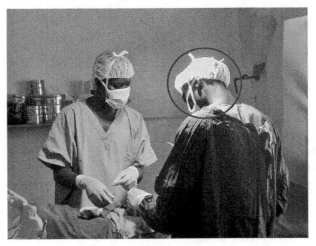

Performing a surgery in South Sudan.

Taking a moment to relax on a mission trip.

With two members of my accountability team, Northern Ireland.

The woman who was delivered and healed at the refugee camp,
northern Kenya.

At a refugee camp in northern Kenya.

With a prayer partner after
my imprisonment in Yemen.

Sharing the love of Jesus, Sudan.

I love teaching and discipling others.

Gordon Mboya, who helped
take care of me in Nairobi.

With my dear brother in Christ, Ibrahim, in Morocco.

Together with Ibrahim and three "men of peace," Middle East.

With a "man of peace" in Eretria.

Praying with indigenous
people during my travels.

With our medical team outside
a Unite 4 Africa medical center, Kenya.

Alongside three "men of peace" in northern Africa.

With a new believer in Jesus Christ, Ahamed. Middle East.

Dickson (middle) and his prayer team. They brought me through!

In Afghanistan with two "men of peace."

At the mosque with several "men of peace," Africa.

With Bishop Mark Kegohi in Kenya.

Having dialogue with two "men of peace" in Africa.

With Dr. Pede (right).

Storytelling and drumming in Africa.

With a "man of peace"
in northern Africa.

Having a silly moment with Ruben, who joined me in Pakistan.

In among the people in Africa.

When motorized
transport just won't do!

With my father, Jeck, in Kenya.

With my mother, Judith, in Kenya.

Hand in hand with my brothers in Kenya in 2021: (left to right) David, me, Jack, Tim, Sylas, and John.

The love of my life, Shyla. Pure joy!

Chapter 6

THE JESUS WAY

I was placed on a flight to Dubai, United Arab Emirates, and I was there for a day before returning to London, then Belfast. I had started feeling sick before I left Eritrea, and I felt worse upon my arrival back in Northern Ireland, so I decided it was best to rest and recover. While I did, I continued to be haunted by the memories of those who had died at my side in Eritrea, saddened by their deaths yet thrilled by their end-of-life confessions of faith in God.

The Lord not only strengthened me during this time, but He gave me grace to remain steadfast in the vow I had made to Him.

I am willing to die for you, God! If I am to die, I will do so if that is what you require.

I no longer wanted to tell the Lord where I needed to go and what I needed to do. I just wanted to show up and let Him do whatever He desired with me. I didn't care where it was. I had seen God work in amazing ways I'd never seen before. So, my prayer was, "Wherever you lead me, I will go. I want to follow you." No problem or obstacle was going to stop me.

I also kept in touch with Ibrahim, not to share what had happened to me in Eritrea, but to discuss the other "men of peace" contacts he had provided and to focus on where I could go next as God opened the doors for me to do so.

After I had been in Belfast for two weeks, I was recovered,

reenergized, and motivated. I decided it was an ideal time to mobilize different Christians in the United Kingdom, bringing them together to share what God had been doing through me, create a place where I could find emotional support and seek funding for the work of the Lord, and unify them in the process. My desire was for them to become a group that provided accountability for me and the work of the ministry.

As I told them about my experiences—particularly those during my incarceration in Eritrea—I got an unpleasant and discouraging surprise.

Some questioned my story. Others doubted it altogether.

Most of them, who I'd consider to be legalistic, didn't believe that those who confessed Christ right before their deaths in the container were actually saved at all. After all, they insisted, they were Muslims. They hadn't been baptized in water, taken the Holy Communion, or attended a new believer Bible study. They hadn't made amends with the people they had wronged. There was nothing to prove their repentance was genuine.

They felt that my ministry methodology was all wrong as well. It was their opinion that I should've held a formal crusade or offered a class on salvation for those to whom I ministered, whether it was behind bars or in the cities.

All of it made me profoundly sad—and I couldn't help but feel that they were trying to project shame and guilt on me to make me think I was doing it wrong and that I was not good enough. More than that, I hated to see how these different believers, with their own rules for how someone should come to salvation in Christ, were so divided. One person, a woman who was among the Christians I'd brought together, admitted, "I feel sad for you because I see the way people are asking you questions and discrediting what you have witnessed. It can become very discouraging."

She was right. It was, and it made me once more return to

the Bible. It was there I found wisdom to respond to what they were telling me. In Scripture, I saw that when Jesus was tempted by Satan in Matthew 4, He always replied to the devil's words with, "It is written." I also saw that Christ did good everywhere He went, yet the religious people had a different opinion about His methods. Jesus healed the sick and set the captives free, yet the Jewish leaders did not like Him. Still, Christ never shied away from the controversy, and He spoke boldly to the doubters and critics, telling them He was only doing what the Father had sent Him to do.

I also read the story of Christ's death, and the final moments of His crucifixion when He was executed along with two other criminals. They were on their own crosses, one on each side of His. The Apostle Luke wrote of this moment, "One of the criminals who hung there hurled insults at him: 'Aren't you the Messiah? Save yourself and us!' But the other criminal rebuked him. 'Don't you fear God,' he said, 'since you are under the same sentence? We are punished justly, for we are getting what our deeds deserve. But this man has done nothing wrong.' Then he said, 'Jesus, remember me when you come into your kingdom.' Jesus answered him, 'Truly I tell you, today you will be with me in paradise.'" (Luke 23:39-43)

Through the Jesus way, people can come to salvation at any place, at any time.

The criminal on the cross never had a chance to do any of the things that many of those Christians I'd brought together believed were necessary for salvation—but Jesus told the man that he would be in heaven with Him that very same day.

That man was saved the Jesus way.

Those who had confessed Christ before they died in that hot container in Eritrea were saved the Jesus way.

Through the Jesus way, people can come to salvation at

any place, at any time, and without any other prerequisites or pre-qualifications. He met and saved people where they were. No conditions. No loopholes.

I liked the Jesus way.

That experience with the different Christians in the United Kingdom, and some other missionaries I had met previously, taught me that religious people will always kill a vision that does not fit their system, model, or way.

I vowed then and there to do things the Jesus way, depend on Him, and follow Him. I wasn't going to care whether or not others liked the story of my life or agreed with it. Jesus kept doing what the Father had called Him to do because He wanted to please the Father, not people. I vowed to please my Father and go where He led me. I was sure there were going to be some places I didn't want to go—but God had proven that, in all circumstances, He would do things in a way I didn't seek or understand.

His way.

I wanted His way—and I wanted to hear Jesus say, "Well done, good and faithful servant," on Judgment Day.

That became my goal, and it took me back to the song I used to sing as a boy.

"I have decided to follow Jesus. No turning back. No turning back."

Ibrahim and I continued to communicate by email and by phone, and in the course of those exchanges, I introduced the possibility of him accompanying me to go and meet the other "men of peace" he had set up for me to visit. In a later phone call, I asked him, "Would you be okay to make a trip with me to meet the friends you've introduced me to?"

I wasn't ready for his response. "I would be glad to, but if I go with you, what would be the mission? They are still my friends, but some of them don't really know the details of what God is doing in me. They only know the stories I've shared."

"You will be going with me as a witness of Christ," I told him.

He was direct. "I don't want to do that."

Convinced it was God's way for him to join me, I offered, "Why don't you just go with me to introduce me to them so I can get to know them because they are your friends? Let's say that you are taking me on a world tour."

I recapped that phone conversation in an email, and Ibrahim agreed to that. Over the next two weeks, we worked out the details and scheduled to meet personally in Paris, France to begin our journey. Admittedly, I was a little anxious as I arrived, worried that Ibrahim might decide to cancel at the last minute or miss his flight. But the second I saw him, all my doubts went away, and I instantly knew that it was God's plan for Ibrahim to go with me. I also understood that I had a true friend in Ibrahim. He was willing, committed, and took action to be there.

Our first stop was Pakistan, followed by Lebanon, Syria, Iran, Yemen, the United Arab Emirates, Somalia, Algeria, and Morocco. I had been to some of the places previously either by myself or with Tearfund, and Ibrahim and I spent a couple of days in Paris to debrief our travels and refresh before flying to Morocco for the first time since I first met him and prayed for his son. It was important to me to make sure I wasn't going to get myself or Ibrahim in trouble when we returned there. I had been told when I was released from prison to never return to Morocco again. I knew it was a risk. But I also knew I was led by the Lord, had faith in Him, and that, this time around, I was also traveling with Ibrahim.

Assured, we went to Morocco and ended up meeting with some of Ibrahim's family as well as other people he had reached out to in Morocco since the last time I was there. I shared my story, and the Lord protected us. Not only were there were no incidents, but I was even able to go into the homes of some of Ibrahim's other family members and friends I had not met the first time to share stories from the Bible, discuss those stories, and then help those people become disciples for Jesus. I did this by creating both discipleship groups and Bible storytelling groups at homes and other safe places, so they could meet together to discover truth from the Bible.

The "world tour" took six weeks, and at every place, Ibrahim introduced me to the "men of peace" he had recommended. The visits were incredible. Because Ibrahim was with me, I didn't have to spend a lot of time introducing myself or my story. Ibrahim did that for me. He spoke about who he was as a Muslim, how he had met me, and what God had done for him and his family. That set the stage for me to share more.

In the end, Ibrahim was a witness for Christ after all, and a powerful one. Having him with me made everything easier, and walls that could've separated me from the others were broken down before I said a single word. His testimony only added to my credibility. I hadn't experienced that previously anywhere else.

I had no difficulties and was not in any danger because of Ibrahim's presence and the relationships he helped to create. He was highly respected by his friends, who were businessmen and Islamic clergymen, and Ibrahim was a true "man of peace" for me. It reminded me of how Jesus went around teaching from village to village, sending out His disciples "two by two" and giving them authority (Mark 6:7). I felt the power of that two by two methodology with Ibrahim during our world tour—and I continue to see how the teamwork and power of two can encourage those who walk together in ministry. It's exactly as Ecclesiastes 4:9 says: "Two are better than one, because they have a good return for their labor."

I had raised enough funds for the trip from previous and new well-wishers and friends who supported me financially. Ibrahim, his business, and his friends also provided significant aid. Plus, during the entire tour with Ibrahim, I also met people in the other countries who I came to consider as "people of peace." Some were friends of Ibrahim's friends or his business associates. Others were individuals, including women, who came to visit with us during our stays in those different places. Most of them were not even believers in Jesus, but God touched their hearts to support me and the ministry.

I was determined to continue building friendships, networks, and a growing movement to enable the continuation of the mission and outreach God had called me to do.

The words that I had spoken to myself as a youth resonated with me stronger than ever.

I want to go.

Right after the world tour was over, Ibrahim and I stayed in Paris for another period of debriefing. I had a list of questions for us to review. When I asked Ibrahim what it was God had showed him about himself during the trip, he responded, "I am not only a follower of Jesus, but I've come to realize that I am His disciple and witness."

He understood the glorious truth that one does not have to go through a discipleship class or program to be considered a disciple of Jesus. All of us who are believers in Christ *are* His disciples. We just have to go and do what He tells us to do.

When I asked Ibrahim if there was anything about the experience that surprised him, he immediately talked about what happened while we were in Lebanon. The second day we were there, Ibrahim asked me to baptize him in the Beirut River. He was amazed at how God had compelled him to be baptized, and it was my joy to do that with him. I baptized Ibrahim at a lovely spot close to where the river met the Mediterranean Sea—and Ibrahim asked the son of one of the Islamic preachers we visited, a young man named Suleiman, to take a photo and video of the occasion so Ibrahim could show it to his family and friends when he returned home.

When I got out of the water, I asked Suleiman, who was with us the entire three days we were in Beirut, Lebanon, "Do you want to be baptized?"

He didn't hesitate. "Yes."

I led him in a prayer of repentance, took him into the river, and baptized him as well.

At the debriefing, Ibrahim told me that one of his biggest challenges during the trip was not knowing what I was going to do next that might be risky or dangerous, and he cited that moment as an example. He was concerned that my decision to ask Suleiman if he wanted to be baptized, and then leading him to Christ and doing the baptism, was going to have negative consequences later. After all, Suleiman was the son of an Islamic preacher. "Why did you decide to baptize him?" Ibrahim asked.

I took him to the Bible's words in Mark 16:15-18, where Jesus said, "Go into all the world and preach the gospel to all creation. Whoever believes and is baptized will be saved, but whoever does not believe will be condemned. And these signs will accompany those who believe: In my name they will drive out demons; they will speak in new tongues; they will pick up snakes with their hands; and when they drink deadly poison, it will not hurt them at all; they will place their hands on sick people, and they will get well."

I explained to Ibrahim that this passage compelled me to directly ask Suleiman to be baptized, just as Ibrahim was compelled by God to be baptized. I did not want Suleiman to miss his opportunity to be baptized because he had heard us declare God's love and salvation since he'd joined us.

I told Ibrahim that I try to always offer that invitation to anyone with whom I come in contact, adding that whenever the truth of Jesus Christ is presented in power, it is accompanied by an undeniable authority. The forces of darkness simply cannot stand in the face of the power and authority of Jesus when we present it.

The forces of darkness simply cannot stand in the face of the power and authority of Jesus.

Ibrahim thought about it and seemed to understand. Then he said, "I've noticed, in every country, that you talk with the people we've visited and ask so many questions to know and understand them, and I really appreciate that. But why do you want to know about the governing laws and the prison situation in each place we visit?"

"One of my heroes in the Bible is the Apostle Paul," I responded, "and he spent a lot of time in jail during his ministry. He showed that, in many ways, it is easier to go into prison and share about Jesus than it is outside of jail." I took Ibrahim in Scripture to Paul's words in 2 Timothy 2:8, where he wrote, "Remember Jesus Christ, raised from the dead, descended from David. This is my gospel, for which I am suffering even to the point of being chained like a criminal. But God's word is not chained. Therefore I endure everything for the sake of the elect, that they too may obtain the salvation that is in Christ Jesus, with eternal glory."

I told Ibrahim, "I have come to realize that even if I go to prison again, in prison God's Word is not chained. I can still proclaim it!" Today, I personally refer to this as "prison ministry," even though my definition of that term is far different from how most others believe prison ministry operates.

Next, I shared Paul's words recorded in Acts 20:22-24. "And now, compelled by the Spirit, I am going to Jerusalem, not knowing what will happen to me there. I only know that in every city the Holy Spirit warns me that prison and hardships are facing me.

However, I consider my life worth nothing to me; my only aim is to finish the race and complete the task the Lord Jesus has given me—the task of testifying to the good news of God's grace."

"Jesus says we will face challenges because of His name," I said to Ibrahim. "That's part of who we should be as His disciples." During that debriefing, I shared other Bible passages with Ibrahim—Acts 21:13 and Ephesians 6:19-20 among them—all to encourage him in his faith and help him to better understand why I was so passionate to see people come to know Christ as their Lord, no matter the cost.

After our briefing was completed, I went to Morocco with Ibrahim to again meet with the discipleship and Bible storytelling groups that were established there earlier in the tour. Afterwards, I headed back to Northern Ireland, where I stayed for the next week. Next, I traveled to Kenya and East Africa for six weeks to rest, visit with people from the churches there who were already part of my support team, and encourage them to continue the good work they were doing in their communities.

I also started planning to return alone to many of the countries I had just visited with Ibrahim. I contacted both the "men of peace" and "people of peace" by email or by phone to make arrangements for future visits. I also contacted those in countries I'd been to before the world tour for the same reason. It encouraged me to see that there was more interest in and questions about God—how the God I serve is different from Allah, or how Jesus can be the Son of God and human (the Son of Man) at the same time—giving me the opportunity to continue discipling those people via phone or email, pray for them, and make plans to return to them.

When I arrived back in Northern Ireland, I had two priorities. First, I worked to reenergize and mobilize those in Sudan and parts of Chad who remained after others had been displaced or killed by the Janjaweed militia terrorist group. Some were considered to be IDPs, while others were refugees in Ethiopia and Northern Kenya. I had overseen the birth of a ministry in Sudan called Cushite 4 Christ Outreach that now had to be reorganized because of the violence.

Second, I launched United for Africa (what would eventually become Unite 4 Africa), in part to provide a ministry home for those still laboring with Cushite 4 Christ and other network partners, but also to fulfill the greater vision God had now given me: mobilize, unite, and equip individuals, communities, and organizations to transform themselves spiritually, socially, physically, and economically, bringing abundant life in Christ to their people.

The name of the organization, and its identification with Africa in particular, came from two things: one practical, the other prophetic. Practically speaking, wherever I went, people first and foremost wanted to know where I was from. I quickly came to see that people associated me with Africa. So, even though my ministry wasn't limited to only African countries, it made sense to brand what I did with Africa.

Prophetically, God gave me a specific directive. If someone looks at the shape of the African continent, it looks like a big footprint. The Lord told me His foot was in Africa, and He wanted Unite 4 Africa to take the feet of Jesus to the uttermost parts of the earth. I thought the imagery was beautiful and powerful.

In addition, as I looked at Scripture, it was clear that God's power had always been manifested in or through Africa. From the stories of Abram (later Abraham) going to Egypt to escape famine, to Joseph being taken captive to Egypt, to Moses and the miraculous liberation of the Israelites from Pharaoh to journey through northern Africa to the Promised Land, and to Jesus Himself fleeing to Egypt to escape death from the jealous King Herod and being raised in Africa to launch His brief ministry that would change mankind forever, it was clear.

Africa was essential to God's past, present, and future work on the earth.

Transformation and revival would take place in and through Africa to reach the entire world as we united together to help bring His purposes to pass. As just one evidence of this, two men that accepted Christ as Lord while I was with them in prison in Eritrea, Jemal and Tesfay, and another I met in that prison who became a Christian after I left, Sheshy, are today part of Unite 4 Africa and have planted churches in Eritrea, Ethiopia, and underground churches in Somalia.

What was seen as loss in the eyes of man in that prison in Eritrea has become great gain for the Kingdom of God! That, too, is the Jesus way.

As of 2021, no fewer than 87 nations worldwide were being directly impacted by Unite 4 Africa. I can't recognize everyone whose tireless, sacrificial service has made that possible because there are so many. In extremely difficult conditions in Yemen, I am thankful that my older brother, John, continues his work there on a medical mission. There are others in Yemen who are planting underground churches while Faisal Ali, Adnan Hassan, and Emir Wadi are mobilizing people in Yemen through our community health empowerment (CHE) program. It's an equipping tool to help communities identify the economic, social, spiritual, and physical problems they are facing and mobilize their own resources to achieve positive and sustainable change. These efforts ultimately lead to the creation of discipleship groups as part of our ongoing disciple making movement.

In Saudi Arabia, Majid, Saleh, and Ahmed are doing an outreach in undisclosed locations called Mosque For The Lord in which they empower people spiritually by discussing the Koran and the Bible with others. In Syria, Farid and Hussein are working with refugees from Iraq while sharing the love of Christ and doing discipleship work in various Syrian communities. In Pakistan, we are working with Habib, Ibrahim, and Azad, who are working to plant underground church communities to empower people with the truth of God's Word. In the United Arab Emirates, Tarek, Faisal, and Saif are leaders working underground to share Christ through their efforts in business.

In Lebanon, Suleiman remains one of our key leaders as a highly respected and outspoken believer in Jesus. He works along-side three people I had the privilege of meeting and discipling: Amal, Mahmoud, and Ridah. Finally, in Morocco, we have no fewer than 100 leaders doing Bible studies, storytelling in the market center, and growing house churches. Those leaders include Khalid, Nasser, Saad, and a few members of Ibrahim's family.

Unite 4 Africa is now headquartered in the United States (Tucson, Arizona), where we train people to be able to go to whatever places the Lord leads them. With every person, I feel like I am going with them to those places as I empower them with the tools to reach people in a contextualized, cultural way— the Jesus way.

We specialize in equipping believers in Christ in cross-cultural studies. When we share the love of Christ with people in other cultures, we want to present the gospel in a relevant way that will best communicate to them. For example, there are some communities where you shouldn't gesture with your hands or show the bottoms of your feet as you are telling a story because to do so would be seen as disrespectful or insulting. We strive to follow the principle Paul set down for us in 1 Corinthians 9:20 when he said, "To the Jews I became like a Jew, to win the Jews. To those under the law I became like one

> I empower them with the tools to reach people in a contextualized, cultural way— the Jesus way.

under the law (though I myself am not under the law), so as to win those under the law."

Through Unite 4 Africa, we also equip people on community health evangelism and empowerment, and we provide tools on how to form and do small group discipleship groups. This is totally different from the traditional way of doing a crusade.

My life and ministry teammate, my wife, Shyla, demonstrates how the training we provide is also effective in how we can serve others in our own communities in the States. She spends time building relationships with a variety of women in her community to dig into issues of reconciliation and spiritual wholeness. She joins people where they are, meeting the needs at hand, and has dialogue with them to draw them to Christ. It is pure discipleship that also then equips these women to use what they have received to disciple others.

Shyla also travels to equip and train women across Africa using Women's Cycle of Life, just one of our ministry and discipling tools to empower women of all ages. Women's Cycle of Life provides biblical teaching and insight on a variety of issues women encounter, from childbirth and menopause to family relationships, forgiveness, and how God values them as individuals.

It's incredible to reflect on what Unite 4 Africa is doing now in light of the incredible work He was doing in me then, even as the ministry was getting underway. The Lord was slowly but persistently bringing me to a whole new level of healing—and He was going to give me some amazing opportunities to forgive others, particularly those who had abused me.

That was coming.

But not until after I endured my most traumatic prison experience of all.

Chapter 7

TO DEATH'S DOOR
AND BACK AGAIN

After the world tour with Ibrahim, I began planning my next
trips and, in the process, debriefing myself on my past journeys and what I had learned from them.

Everywhere I had gone, I was asked the same question: "Why
are Africans poor?" Because I was from Africa, I was tagged with
the label of poverty, and that got me thinking, "What, then, is
poverty?" I saw every kind of poverty everywhere I had been. If
it wasn't financial, it was emotional. If it wasn't emotional, it was
social. If it wasn't social, it was spiritual. If it wasn't spiritual, it was
mental.

I came to define poverty as "an inability to change your situation physically, socially, mentally, spiritually, and emotionally." I
decided I wanted to better address the subject of poverty in my
future trips, tying it to the mission God had already given me for
Unite 4 Africa.

I went to Scripture and found Luke 4:14-19. "Jesus returned
to Galilee in the power of the Spirit, and news about him spread
through the whole countryside. He was teaching in their synagogues, and everyone praised him. He went to Nazareth, where he
had been brought up, and on the Sabbath day he went into the syn-
agogue, as was his custom. He stood up to read, and the scroll of

the prophet Isaiah was handed to him. Unrolling it, he found the place where it is written: 'The Spirit of the Lord is on me, because he has anointed me to proclaim good news to the poor. He has sent me to proclaim freedom for the prisoners and recovery of sight for the blind, to set the oppressed free, to proclaim the year of the Lord's favor.'"

There it was. One of the main reasons Jesus came into the world was to proclaim the good news to the poor—and the poor were present everywhere, with their poverty coming in many forms.

My desire to address poverty fit perfectly with the original vision God had given me. I was even more determined to declare that Jesus, and only Him, was the solution to poverty and the only one who could bring true and lasting transformation to the world.

As I began the process of organizing teams that I could meet with in various churches in Africa, and others in the United Kingdom and United States who could commit to pray for me and the mission, many of them expressed concern that the countries I wanted to visit next carried too high of a risk.

No one wanted to accompany me because of that risk. Others felt I shouldn't go at all.

Either way, most agreed I needed a charity organization under which I should travel and minister, but I disagreed. I wanted to continue doing what my heart was leading me to do, using the Jesus way. I was convinced that as I shared my story, His parables, and engaged others in dialogue with a renewed focus of addressing their physical, social, mental, spiritual, or emotional poverty, more and more people would come to faith in Christ. They could then participate by sharing that good news with their friends and family, just as Ibrahim had. As a result, I could organize discipleship groups with those people, and that would lead to a greater discipleship movement.

I left Northern Ireland, stayed in Turkey for a day, then traveled to Yemen, Egypt, Lebanon, and back to London for two days before going to Iran, Jordan, and Saudi Arabia. In each country, I met with the "men of peace" introduced to me previously by Ibrahim or with the "people of peace" I'd met during my time with Tearfund. In each place, I met with someone I trusted to be my translator and travel companion to fulfill the two-by-two teamwork approach Jesus used with His disciples. Some were welcoming, but there was increased conflict with most because I was more open than before in speaking about Jesus and how He was the solution to all forms of poverty. Many never accepted this, asking me to provide a comparison between Jesus and the prophet Muhammad. I was clear. "Yes, God used Muhammad in His own way, but the ultimate person who will change and transform us is Jesus." I received a lot of push back for that, and relationships with some of the men and people of peace faded because they felt I was being too confrontational.

Undeterred, when I went to Iran, my messaging led to a heated dialogue with the "man of peace" who I had previously met with Ibrahim. He was an Islamic leader, though not necessarily a preacher, but he became uncomfortable as I connected with Christians I had met in Tehran, the nation's capital. I was accused of promoting propaganda, picked up by the police, and incarcerated. I was interrogated for three days, given three lashes, and ordered to leave the country.

A similar thing happened next in Jordan. I was accused of being in that country illegally even though I had the proper documents. I was detained, interrogated, and found guilty of sharing religion as a missionary even though I did not possess a permit identifying me as a missionary. I was given the choice to serve one year in prison or get six lashes and pay a fine. I chose the latter, but then they unexpectedly doubled the lashes, waived the fee, and simply ordered me to leave.

All of it made me that much more determined. I was so stubborn. I was not going to stop, no matter what happened.

I remembered what I thought as a boy when I was preparing to escape the terrorist camp in Uganda, and it still rang true.

If I'm going to die anyway, I would rather die doing something.

After a brief return to London and Northern Ireland, I traveled next to Pakistan. I met with some friends from the United Kingdom who did missionary work in that country, and when I met with the "men of peace" there, I learned about a medical group from Korea who were doing charitable aid work alongside some Pakistani doctors I had also met. Because of my medical background, I connected with them. I stayed with the "men of peace" for two days, and I also visited some friends that I met either through the workers or that I'd known from previous visits.

Abbas, one of the "men of peace," asked me, "What, then, do you want to do while you are here?"

I replied, "I want to proclaim the good news of the Lord."

After a long silence, they asked, "Are you an aid worker?"

I said, "No, I am not an aid worker, but I believe anywhere I go I want to bless people because the good news is here, the Kingdom of God is at hand, and Jesus came to proclaim the good news to the poor. I can see that, in this country, there are people who are poor in many ways, and I have seen how Jesus can transform poverty."

"I have seen how Jesus can transform poverty."

I also shared with Abbas what had happened to me in prison previously. "This left me emotionally disturbed and mentally poor because of the pain that I had to go through as a result of the torture," I told him. "But my strength is building, and Jesus is giving me the strength because He is my comfort to continually heal me."

Interestingly, Abbas would later become a Christian. But then, as had happened before, my undeviating message about Jesus began to weaken my relationship with the "men of peace," so I decided to visit the Korean group that was doing mission work. I got to know them well, and Dr. Yao was a great help to me. He enlightened me about what was going on in Pakistan and the high risk that was associated with being there. He also advised me of the extreme risk I was taking by being more direct and transparent about Jesus.

After that, I met with some Pakistanis who were doing an evangelistic radio broadcasting and literature ministry in Karachi, Pakistan, which included medical and music camps where people could share about Jesus and tell Bible stories. They introduced me to some believers who were in Quetta, a city that was about 420 miles directly north of Karachi. So, after spending time with the Pakistanis in Karachi, I went to Quetta. They, too, were doing medical and music camps along with art camps and literacy classes, and I was inspired by their commitment to meet the spiritual needs of the people in Quetta. I was able to use the literacy classes to introduce oral storytelling from the Bible, which was so effective in allowing people to have dialogue and process the accounts from Scripture to discover the truth for themselves. I benefitted even more as I began learning Urdu, the official language of Pakistan, through my interpreter as I shared the Bible stories with the people.

As I saw some of the wonderful prison ministry work this group was doing, the discrimination and overwhelming oppression faced by the few minority Christians in Quetta, and Pakistan as a whole, was becoming clear to me. It was greatly disturbing.

One day, about a week after my arrival in Quetta, I was sharing Bible stories with a small group at the medical camp south of the city, I told them how Jesus "went through all the towns and villages, teaching in their synagogues, proclaiming the good news of the kingdom and healing every disease and sickness." (Matthew 9:35) I'd then answer questions about what they learned and further explain what God did through Jesus.

While I was telling the stories about Jesus healing the woman who touched the edge of His cloak (Matthew 9:20-22) and the 10 lepers who called to Him for mercy (Luke 17:12-16), some people arrived to hear what I was saying. I did not know who they were, but they began asking me to compare Jesus with the prophet Muhammad—and, just as I had done so many times before, I firmly stated my belief in Christ as the Savior of mankind, declared how He healed many who had faith and believed in Him, and proclaimed how He had healed me whenever I needed it. "Today, He will still heal whoever puts their trust in Him," I said.

The next day, I was arrested at the medical camp along with two of my Pakistani translators, Yousuf and Nazir. Though I tried to find out what they were charged with, I was never able to learn what happened to them, but I was accused of blasphemy against Muhammad—and specifically of making derogatory remarks about him, though I didn't feel that was necessarily true with what I had said. I was found guilty of spreading the teachings of Jesus, and because of the structure of their justice system at that time, I was not required to appear before a judge. I was immediately transferred to a detention facility.

I don't know exactly where I was taken for further interrogation, but I was incarcerated along with some of the other Pakistanis who had hosted me during my visit. There were nine of us in all. We were whipped before being forced to watch a video.

We looked on in horror as we saw a few people, who our captors said were followers of Jesus, being placed into a brick kiln.

Their hands bound, they were thrown in alive and burned.

"That will be the punishment for you infidels," one of the jailers told us.

Our group was then separated into three smaller ones, and we remained separated until the two times each day that we were allowed to gather to pray with one another. For the next three days, we were constantly interrogated and whipped. We were considered to be nothing more than infidels awaiting our punishment. In all, I was moved to four different facilities—and everywhere I went, I was surprised to find that Christians made up the vast majority of the prisoners.

Oddly, it was refreshing because we were allowed to talk and pray with one another. I thought it was strange that they'd call us infidels, yet still allow us to worship as followers of Christ. We called it "God's mystery." We were also given permission to sing and worship together, so long as we didn't get too loud.

I should've honored that limitation, but I didn't. I joined a few others in boldly and loudly praising Jesus. Not long after that, three of us were gathered, handcuffed, taken away, and placed in a large containment room with a metal grill around it that looked like prison bars but was more like a giant cage.

In that room, there was a single video camera and people wearing hoods.

One of them held a long and presumably sharp sword.

We were ordered to kneel.

"Because you have blasphemed the holy prophet Muhammad, you must be punished. You are going to give a statement on video for your families and fellow infidels before you receive your punishment."

They weren't mean or angry when they said it. It was so matter-of-fact, as though the act of execution—and our lives—meant nothing to them.

I shuddered, thinking we were going to be taken away and burned alive. I started to figure out what I was going to say. *This is going to be my only chance to talk them out of it and spare my life.*

The first inmate, a British man, pleaded for his life. "I have a family! I will never do this again, and I agree that the Holy Prophet is the last Messenger of God!"

Thhip!

His head was chopped off right in front of us. Blood spurted and pooled below his prone torso.

Bile rose in my throat as the second man, a Pakistani, was told to give his statement. In rapid Arabic, he, too, begged to live and pledged to never again blaspheme the prophet.

Thhip!

His head hit the floor and rolled to the right. His blood flowed and mingled with the other ichor already on the floor.

No. I'm not going to be burned alive. I'm going to be beheaded!

My heart seemed ready to pound out of my chest as the man with the sword took his position behind me. *I'm going to die right here—right now.*

I was ordered to speak. I had thought about what I was going to say.

But that wasn't what came out of my mouth.

"I don't have much to record," I began as strongly as I could muster. "I am so thankful that I'm here. I'm so thankful that you will take this initiative to promote me to go be with my Lord and family in heaven. I am so glad because I'll never go through this pain and punishment again here on earth. I'm thankful for God and for you to be the link to take me where I'll never suffer. To Him be the glory, and I'm ready to go to heaven and have my reward, eternal life."

I closed my eyes and wondered if there would be any pain.

There was—but it was from a sharp kick in the ribs.

As I doubled over, someone grabbed my pants and dragged me out of the room.

Overcome, I blacked out.

When I came to, I was all alone in another cage. In the intense trauma of the moment, I didn't know what to expect. I wondered why my life had been spared. Had it been done just so they could incinerate me later in the brick kiln? Was there some other reason? I had no idea, and whenever I pleaded with God for answers, I didn't get any.

All I knew was that I was alive, and that was enough.

My memories of the rest of the incarceration remain elusive to this day—but I received more beatings, including having a long, thin needle stuck into my testicles. It was excruciating. The pain stung all the way up into my head, and I have never felt anything like that before or since. The damage caused by the abuse made me wonder if I'd ever be able to someday father children.

> All I knew was that I was alive, and that was enough.

A few days later, I was released and returned to a police station in Karachi. I have no recollection of how I was sent away. I only recall that two days later, I was put on a plane to Egypt, then to Turkey, and then another one that took me to London.

I could not get the image of that hot, burning fire in the brick kiln out of my mind until I was safely seated on the first flight out.

I was quite ill when I arrived back in Belfast. Dickson Mac-Gregor, a friend and prayer partner, took good care of me over the next two weeks. He was such a blessing. My Bible never made it back with me from Pakistan, but for that first week home, I did not read a Bible—and I didn't care to ask for one. Mentally and emotionally drained, I struggled greatly with nightmares as I relived my trauma. I heard voices. Even fully awake, I could see my captors coming to behead me or throw me into the fire.

I felt isolated, fearful, and lonely. There was pain, rejection, abandonment, and anger and rage that fed a deep hatred toward people and even God. I was gripped with anxiety and guilt that came from frustration, self-pity, discouragement, and hopelessness. I constantly thought of suicide.

As much as I wanted to be positive, knowing that God had again somehow rescued me from certain death, I found myself overflowing with negativity about anything and everything.

Most of all, I was confused about why I did not die with my fellow brothers, who I saw as being heroes of the gospel. I cried whenever I remembered our conversations and fellowship together in prison before they were beheaded. My memories of them today bring even more sorrow to my heart.

Being alive meant nothing to me at that moment. I wished I could die. I struggled to concentrate, and I did not reach out to anyone or read any of my emails. I could not move well because of the beatings and trauma, so I mostly stayed in bed.

I was not honest with Dickson about what had happened to me, but I could tell he knew something wasn't right. I most appreciated how he graciously gave me my space, knowing that it would be just a matter of time before I opened up and shared things with him. Dickson was patient and grateful that I was with him, even if we did not pray like we usually did whenever we were together. How could I possibly pray? The memories of all my past suffering came flooding back to me—pain I thought I had already dealt with.

So did the questions. "Why am I doing what I am doing?" "Is there anything good about being a disciple of Jesus or following through on the vision He gave me?"

I kept encountering the same traumatic situations after praying that God would never have me go through them again.

Why?

I had lost myself and lost control of who I was.

That was probably the longest two weeks of my life.

As Dickson began to ask me what my next plans were, I didn't know, and he was kind enough to reach out to my prayer networks and accountability team on my behalf. I do not remember much of what I said to Dickson, but when he asked me what I needed, I replied, "If I can get a Bible, that would be great."

He found one, brought it to me, and that night, I found the answer to some of my questions. I reluctantly opened the Bible and landed on Matthew 10—and as I read, verse by precious verse, I began to cry. I started to worship the Lord from the innermost depths of my soul. In verse 16, Jesus told His beloved disciples, "I am sending you out like sheep among wolves. Therefore be as shrewd as snakes and as innocent as doves."

Snakes? Doves? I am more like a sheep—a dumb, stupid sheep.

I smiled, probably for the first time in days, as I thought back to my childhood in Kenya. Whenever I would go out into the forest to tend to the sheep, goats, and other animals, and the hyenas attacked, the goats always cried out, but the sheep didn't. In fact, they'd do nothing at all to ward off the attack. When I asked my brothers why that was the case, Jack said of the sheep, "Their brains aren't working right. Even when there is a threat, they'll just walk right into it. They have a rotten brain, the stupidest of all, but they are loyal."

Is that how I am? I wondered. *Is that why I keep getting into trouble and going back to prison, even when I know what could happen? Maybe my brain isn't working right.*

Then I recalled the story of the Good Shepherd and His sheep from John 10. *Sheep can do nothing without their shepherd. Their brains are rotten and useless. Yet the shepherd—Jesus, the Good Shepherd—would give His life to save His sheep.*

To save me.

Maybe I am like a dumb sheep, but in a good way—for Jesus.

I read on in Matthew 10, and each word was like healing salve to my spirit. Then I came to verses 19-20. "But when they arrest you, do not worry about what to say or how to say it. At that time you will be given what to say, for it will not be you speaking, but the Spirit of your Father speaking through you."

That's when I knew that the words that I had said to my would-be executioners in Pakistan were not my own. They were the words of the Holy Spirit. I realized *that* was the moment that Scripture was fulfilled in my life.

It reassured me once more of the vision God had given me, and of my determination to fulfill it.

I wept and allowed God's Word and His Spirit to become medicine to my soul, mind, and spirit. Wiping away the tears, I kept reading. "So do not be afraid of them, for there is nothing concealed that will not be disclosed, or hidden that will not be made known." (verse 26) "Do not be afraid of those who kill the body but cannot kill the soul. Rather, be afraid of the One who can destroy both soul and body in hell." (verse 28) "So don't be afraid; you are worth more than many sparrows." (verse 31)

Each passage brought such great relief from my pain when I was bound with fear. They began to shift my mindset and renew hope and life within me. As short as the verses were, I read each one over and over again—and the voice of His truth spoke louder than the voices of my trauma.

Then came Matthew 10:32-33, and it was as though I could hear the voice of Jesus Himself speaking the words directly to me.

"Whoever acknowledges me before others, I will also acknowledge before my Father in heaven. But whoever disowns me before others, I will disown before my Father in heaven."

I broke into more tears and began crying and praying aloud, just as I had done in that Pakistan prison before I was taken into that horrific containment room.

Dickson heard me, came in, and joined me. We wept and worshipped together at the top of our voices for hours. All of the pain, anguish, and hurt was breaking in me, from me, and away from me. Dickson had a full-time job and lots of responsibilities, but he cancelled everything for the next three days to focus solely on being with me. Dickson and I read more from the Bible, and the Lord used His Word to minister to me at my deepest point of need.

We also began praying, and we had intermittent times of being completely quiet, listening to the Lord, and hearing what He was speaking to us.

This kind of listening prayer is not formulaic. It can take minutes, hours, or days. Often, God will use it to reveal a lie that we have heard or believed about a specific area He wants us to address in our lives, and then He'll speak the truth to us. That brings a new and deeper form of healing that can lead to forgiveness of ourselves or others.

God mightily used Dickson, and he eventually called four other friends who took me through more needed time of healing and recovery. Dickson was a prayer warrior and intercessor, and he rallied friends like Paul Wilbur, who was on tour with Pray for the Peace of Jerusalem, and other friends to lead me through healing prayers and moments of deep, intimate worship, the likes of which I had never experienced before.

During these three days of specific and intensive times of prayer, I discovered that I had not even begun to deal with some of my past struggles. Still, God kept speaking to me and affirming His vision to use me to the uttermost parts of the world. He told me He had done what He had done, and He was not done with me yet. I heard Him clearly speak to me that I would return to Pakistan and all the other places I had been.

I remember the prayers I made that day. "I give myself away so you can use me. Use me as you will. Here I am, here I stand, Lord. My life is in your hands, and I am longing to see your desires revealed in and through me. I give myself away. Take my heart, take my life as a living sacrifice. All my dreams and plans, Lord, I place them in your hands. To you I belong. My life is not my own, and I give myself away."

ABDUCTED BUT NOT FORSAKEN

Dickson led the prayer team to sing a song over me using those words. It was a deeply emotional time.

I vowed anew to serve the Lord no matter what—knowing my rewards waiting in Heaven were greater than anything I could face or go through here on earth.

It was truly amazing.

> I vowed anew to serve the Lord no matter what.

Refreshed, I began updating those who had been supporting my ministry, and I started following up with those in the countries I had previously visited. I also resumed reaching out to other "people of peace" I had yet to meet. My network grew, and the Lord blessed me and provided for my needs.

Finally, I began working on how I could strategically follow God's leading while better honoring the mandate from Jesus in Matthew 10:17 where He told His disciples to "be on your guard; you will be handed over to the local councils and be flogged in the synagogues." I prayed not to be naïve, but still be ready to do whatever God wanted to do with me in obedience to Matthew 10:38-39, which says, "Whoever does not take up their cross and follow me is not worthy of me. Whoever finds their life will lose it, and whoever loses their life for my sake will find it." I did not want to fear losing my life for His sake, knowing my reward was in heaven.

I reconnected with a friend in London, Dr. Paul Howarth, who I had previously met at Kijabe Mission Hospital in Kenya. I did not share with him the details of what had happened to me in Pakistan and the other places I had visited. Because the memories of recent my trauma were still so powerful, I didn't want to be misunderstood or rejected by him or anyone else who disagreed with what I had chosen to do. But we did talk about some of the stories we had shared when we met in Kijabe with Dr. Richard Bransford. I had traveled with Richard into southern Sudan and Somalia to help serve children with disabilities.

In our conversation, Paul told me about a group in Afghanistan doing medical outreach work and discipleship. Paul said he had thought about going there but did not feel called by God to do so. I told him about my previous visits to that country when I traveled with Tearfund, and I asked Paul if he'd connect me with the people he knew there.

As I thought back to what I had just been through in Pakistan, I drew courage from Matthew 10:22-23, where Jesus told His disciples, "You will be hated by everyone because of me, but the one who stands firm to the end will be saved. When you are persecuted in one place, flee to another. Truly I tell you, you will not finish going through the towns of Israel before the Son of Man comes."

The disciples and the Apostle Paul did not stop when they were released from imprisonments. They did not stop when they had been persecuted.

Neither could I.

I want to go.

Without thinking to take more time to rest from my ordeal in Pakistan or the encounter with God that followed in Belfast, I decided I had to travel to Afghanistan as soon as possible. Once I was there in the capital city of Kabul, I met with some "men of peace" I knew through Ibrahim and from my previous visit with Tearfund, and I also learned more about the work being done there by the group Paul had mentioned. I joined them in Ghazni, Afghanistan, a three-hour drive southwest of Kabul. With the goal of volunteering with them, I observed how they were serving the people and sharing the good news. My plan was to remain in Afghanistan for about six weeks, and I wanted to spend some of that time serving with them.

Though the group was affiliated with the Korean Presbyterian church, no one there was allowed to talk about Jesus Christ. As in so many other places in the Middle East, to do so in Afghanistan was dangerous. It is also a place where Sharia law is strictly enforced, and officials are watching everything you say and do.

After three days in Ghazni, I returned to Kabul to visit with three other "men of peace," one of whom I had met before and two others that had been introduced to me by Ibrahim. My time with these "men of peace" was mostly cordial, and they asked lots of questions about where I was from, how I had come to visit Afghanistan, and about my religious beliefs. They wanted to engage in dialogue to get to know me and understand me. For the next five days, I chose to go with them to the mosques, and I took part with them in Islamic prayers. They were open to having me pray for them, but they made it clear that Christian faith and talking about the Bible was not tolerated.

I remembered what I had read in Matthew 10:16-17: "I am sending you out like sheep among wolves. Therefore be as shrewd as snakes and as innocent as doves. Be on your guard; you will be handed over to the local councils and be flogged in the synagogues." I tried to not proclaim the gospel openly, but basically speak it out when I prayed. One time when I was praying with one of the "men of peace" who was an Islamic preacher, I brought in the words from John 8:32 and John 14:6. "And God, your Word says that we shall know the truth and the truth shall set you free," I prayed. "May this truth continuously be revealed to me and to others around me, that we maybe be free from any affliction, bondage, fears, or anything that does not give you the glory that belongs to you alone. Thank you for truth, and you are the way, the truth, and the life. Amen."

A couple of hours later, the preacher invited me into his prayer room for coffee time, a daily ritual in Middle Eastern countries where people stop to gather, sit, and visit with one another.

"What is the truth that you mentioned in your prayers?" he asked me. "Is truth a person?"

He had told me there was to be no discussion about my faith and the Bible, and yet now he is initiating the dialogue?

"Well," I replied calmly, "I am not afraid to share in relation to your question, but would you promise to not categorize it as Christian faith, but as my lifestyle and belief?"

He agreed. I said, "Prophet Jesus said in the Scripture that He is the way and the truth and the life, and that no one goes to the Father our God above except through believing in Him, the Prophet Jesus."

He didn't say anything, and in the silence that followed I started to think the worst was about to happen. Nervously, I said, "You promised not to—"

He quietly interrupted, "I want to talk and reason with you more about that."

To this day, Sheikh Abdallah, that "man of peace," is still my friend, and we talk and have dialogue about the Bible without any conditions. We love each other even though He is still a Muslim and not yet a follower of Christ. Through him, I have met other people who have given their lives to Jesus and are quietly and secretly following His teachings there in Afghanistan. I am amazed at how the Lord works—the Jesus way.

Next, I went back to Ghazni. I served the Korean medical missionaries in their medical camp, seeing sick people but not sharing any Bible stories. They had a center where ill people came for treatment, and I learned things from the Korean doctors I had not known before.

One evening, a man was brought in, his shirt soaked with blood. His arm had been cut off. We didn't know why, but we assumed it was possible he was convicted as a thief and his arm had been amputated in accordance with Sharia law.

Without hesitation, we treated his wounds. As we helped him, the man confirmed our suspicions—and, also without hesitation, I took the opportunity to tell him about Jesus Christ, of how He came to deliver the poor and oppressed, and of how salvation was available only through Him. I did this because it was late at night and the security people who would normally be listening in were away and asleep. In addition, I used an interpreter to communicate since I could not speak the man's language, which was either Pashto or Dari, the two official languages of Afghanistan.

The man gave his life to the Lord that very night.

The next day, the police came to the clinic.

The man was still there in recovery, and the police asked us why we had treated him, telling us he had been convicted as a thief. "We don't know anything about that," others responded. That's when the man spoke up, admitting that he was a thief but had been scared to say anything about it the night before.

I had to say something.

"The man being a thief really doesn't matter. What matters is that he was a patient. Whether he was on the wrong side of the law or not is none of our business. We're going to do what God does, and God is about the lost and sinners receiving compassion."

I could see that those around me were annoyed by my words, but I continued.

"Not only did we try to rescue him, we wanted to rescue his soul. If he is a sinner and a thief, then leading him to Christ, repenting of his sin, and accepting Jesus was the best solution for him. He will never be a thief again."

I was immediately taken from the clinic and interrogated further. "Are you here treating people," they asked, "or are you here spreading infidel agendas?"

"Both," I said, "and the priority is their soul being right with the Lord."

My directness and hard-headedness led to me being detained. I was put in jail in Ghazni. After two days, I was transferred to Kabul at Pul-e-Charkhi prison, also known as the Afghan National Detention Facility, the largest prison in Afghanistan. I was questioned, and I was defiant. I was accused of blaspheming the prophet Muhammad and spreading false teaching. I was whipped and beaten.

Because of the trauma I had endured in Pakistan—and despite the lengthy time of worship and prayer with Dickson and the prayer team—I again became bitter, angry, and ready to die.

But, by the grace of God, I didn't want to give up or give in. During one of the interrogations, I told my captors about the three "men of peace," Abdallah, Zahid, and Reshad, who were all sheikhs, and insisted I had not come into Afghanistan illegally or to cause trouble.

"I was their guests, I had stayed in their homes, and I had gone to the mosques to pray when I was with them," I said. "You say that I am an infidel, and I understand that. I did not come to blaspheme Allah or any prophet. I would not have gone to the mosques with my friends if that were true."

I was able to successfully request that the "men of peace" come to the prison to see me and pray for me—and all three did just that. They were highly respected Islamic leaders and businessmen. They told the officials that I had indeed been their guest, that I was a good man, and that when I left them to go to Ghazni, I had done so in good standing.

Their testimony helped secure my release after a week in custody. Upon my release, I stayed with Sheikh Abdallah for three days until there was a flight available to take me out of Afghanistan.

The day before I left the country, I did something I had never done before.

Sheikh Reshad and a few of his leaders made the arrangements and accompanied me as I returned to the prison. Once we arrived, I asked the officials to forgive me for whatever it was they thought I did wrong—and then I forgave them for their treatment of me.

The prison officers did not verbally ask to be forgiven. As far as they were concerned, they had done no wrong. They felt they were abiding by Sharia law, and perhaps their Islamic beliefs did not allow them to process forgiveness like I did.

Nevertheless, one of the prison officers said they had never had anyone return to do that before—and it led to more dialogue that enabled me to say that forgiveness was what Prophet Jesus, my Savior and healer, required me to do so I could leave them in peace. I had the confidence to say what I did because God laid upon my heart to do so. I also knew Sheikh Reshad and his leaders were with me and had already planned my exit from Afghanistan.

It was profound, and when I got on the plane to leave the next day, I truly did feel at peace because of the power of forgiveness shown by me that day in Kabul. I knew that I was leaving on good, godly terms that would ensure I could someday return because I had made friends with the prison officers in Kabul. I was also able to communicate with the Koreans who had hosted me in Ghazni, and I asked them to forgive me for any interference I caused after they had allowed me to volunteer.

Through it all, the "men of peace" became friends with the Korean missionaries and became a great help to them in different ways. It reminded me how all things work together for good to those who love the Lord (Romans 8:28).

That was just the beginning of the healing my amazing God was starting to work within me through forgiveness.

On my way back to London, I started to make plans to return to the places where I had previously gone and been persecuted.

Everything that God was doing only made me love Him more, trust Him more, and commit to giving myself away so He could use me for His glory—no matter what came next.

Chapter 8

A JOURNEY INTO FORGIVENESS

After my return to Belfast, I updated my prayer team, account-ability partners, and supporters. I honestly communicated how gracious God had been with me. Because I had experienced that time of God's intense healing before leaving for Afghanistan, I felt I had more freedom than before to be open with them—allowing me to share more details about my previous suffering, and issues such as fear and depression.

As I got caught up on my email messages, I saw one from a faithful prayer partner and mentor, Bishop Mark Kegohi from Jesus Care Center in Kisumu, Kenya. It simply said, "Call me when you get this message."

I immediately contacted him. He said, "For the past few weeks, we have been praying for you. You have been coming into our hearts during our Friday overnight prayers and weekly morning glory prayers. But since I have not heard from you lately, we don't really know exactly where you are, and more importantly, we don't know why the Lord has placed you repeatedly on our hearts."

"How did that happen?" I asked him. "Which days were you praying?"

Bishop Mark revealed that the days they were praying—the very days God had placed in their hearts—were the same days that

I was in prison in Afghanistan. He also told me that the day I was released was the day when they felt there was victory!

I was incredibly amazed by how God miraculously worked through the Holy Spirit to lead them to pray on the specific days I was going through my greatest challenges, asking the Lord to provide for my safety and for God to glorify Himself in whatever way was needed.

I had not told Bishop Mark or his church leaders anything about my schedule. They had no idea where I was. Yet God heard and answered the prayers of these faithful believers on my behalf.

I was humbled—and because of that, I was more determined to obey the Lord.

Then, another dear friend that I had first met in southern Sudan, a retired American doctor named Ben Button, contacted me by email. As I told him about some of the things that had recently happened to me, he invited me to come to Rochester, New York for a time of rest. He said I could meet his family, perhaps speak at his church, and maybe even tell some of my stories at his church's denominational conference.

I decided to take him up on his offer, and I visited for one month. I'd been in the United States many times before, but this was my first visit to Rochester. Dr. Ben set aside time to drive me to different places in New York, and across the international border into Ottawa, Canada, that I had never seen before. The beauty of the land was wonderful.

Aside from those sightseeing trips, I spent most of my time alone, thinking and praying about how I could go back to the countries where I'd been imprisoned and persecuted. I wrestled with my choice. I didn't know how anything would turn out. I knew there was a chance I could be thrown back in prison. I also knew I could be killed. That terrified me. Yet I also knew God had rescued me out of everything before, and that He would do it again if it were His will.

That made me wonder, *What would happen to the vision the Lord had given me for Unite 4 Africa if I died?*

In the end, I concluded that returning to those places would start a movement—one that would live on without me, even if I was killed for my belief in Jesus. With faith mixed with some fear, I started mobilizing more leaders for Unite 4 Africa who could continue on with the ministry if God, in His plan, allowed others to take my life.

It was also there, in New York, that I began to dig deeper into God's Word and study more about healing and forgiveness.

In Matthew 6, right after the model prayer Jesus gave His disciples, the one we know today as "The Lord's Prayer," I read verses 14-15. Christ warned, "For if you forgive other people when they sin against you, your heavenly Father will also forgive you. But if you do not forgive others their sins, your Father will not forgive your sins."

I knew that I was born a sinner and that I needed God's forgiveness for the sins I commit due to my human nature. Yet those verses were not easy for me to process at first because I was hanging on to my past hurt with a victim mindset. I struggled with the truth that in order to receive God's forgiveness, I had to forgive others. *If I keep holding on to unforgiveness,* I thought, *then I am disobeying God.*

I also understood the consequences of not obeying God's Word and following His instructions in the Bible. I thought of Saul (see 1 Samuel 9-31), who refused to seek the Lord and had God's Spirit taken from him, and David (see 1-2 Samuel and Psalm 51), who confessed his sins, sought God's forgiveness, and received it.

I heard God clearly tell me that forgiveness required an act of obedience to Him and His Word in order for me to receive my own forgiveness from sin and obtain the blessing of healing for my broken and wounded heart.

Then I wondered, *But what about justice? Should those who hurt me also have to suffer pain before I forgive them?*

I heard God clearly tell me that forgiveness required an act of obedience.

God softly responded, using His own Word from 1 Thessalonians 5:15. "Have you not read that no one should pay back evil for evil, but only seek that which is good for each other and everyone else?" With tears, knowing how much I had received God's forgiveness and still needed more, I saw that I had no other choice but to embrace forgiveness. I began taking the lies I had believed when I was in pain and replacing them with God's truth.

I continued reading and came to Ephesians 4:31-32. "Get rid of all bitterness, rage and anger, brawling and slander, along with every form of malice. Be kind and compassionate to one another, forgiving each other, just as in Christ God forgave you." I felt all of those emotions and more when I was imprisoned and being tortured, but this passage encouraged me to forgive and be tenderhearted and merciful to those who had hurt me. No wonder the Bible declares in Micah 7:18-19, "Who is a God like you, who pardons sin and forgives the transgression of the remnant of his inheritance? You do not stay angry forever but delight to show mercy. You will again have compassion on us; you will tread our sins underfoot and hurl all our iniquities into the depths of the sea."

I came to the conclusion that forgiveness required me to be kind, compassionate, and merciful. I wanted to hit back at my abusers, feeling that I was above them, if just for a moment. But Micah showed me a God who showered His love on a rebellious and inconsiderate people. He had every right not to do so, but instead of repaying them with wrath, He extended forgiveness and grace. As His dearly loved child, God expected me to do the same to those who had abused me. It was more truth that shed more light on my need to forgive.

Then I recalled how Peter had asked Jesus, "Lord, how many times shall I forgive my brother or sister who sins against me? Up to seven times?" Christ answered, "I tell you, not seven times, but seventy-seven times." (Matthew 18:21-22) In those days, the rabbis taught that a person must forgive someone else three times, but Christ's response indicated that the amount of times we are to forgive others is limitless.

That revealed that forgiveness required me to be patient, which I believe was the exact lesson Jesus wanted Peter to learn. Later, Paul wrote, "Bear with each other and forgive one another if any of you has a grievance against someone. Forgive as the Lord forgave you." (Colossians 3:13)

Again, I was challenged. *Does bear with each other mean that I have to forgive the unbearable and unkind actions of others?* Dealing with unkind people wasn't easy for me to begin with. *What if my abusers are unbearable and unkind when I meet them again?* Some of my friends and supporters wondered why I would even think of going back to meet those who hurt me, much less forgive them. They doubted God was leading me at all.

Well, I thought, *I lost a few friends and supporters before because of my obedience to return to where I was persecuted.* I could understand how Job must've felt with his friends Eliphaz, Bildad, and Zophar who incessantly accused him during his suffering (see Job chapters 4-27). I recalled again what my brother Jack had said about sheep. *Some of my friends think I am a dumb sheep whose brain isn't working right. They believe I'm out of my mind.*

Nevertheless, I kept learning that forgiveness required my

patience. I determined to keep praying and to wait on God to intervene when I went and met my captors.

The deeper I studied the Bible about forgiveness, the more it became clear that the confession of my own sins was required as well. Yes, I had been sinned against, but I had my sins, too. In 1 John 1:9, I read of God, "If we confess our sins, he is faithful and just and will forgive us our sins and purify us from all unrighteousness." I resigned myself to the fact that I was focusing more on the sins done against me and did not want to consider my own sins. I needed to confess them to the Lord.

In my anger, rage, loneliness, pain, and bitterness, I'd had so many wicked thoughts and attitudes toward others, especially those who had abused me. These were sinful, evil thoughts and wishes, yet that verse broke through all of that and convicted me. I mostly quake at the thought of my own sins, and of how much harder it is to confess them to others. But I was seeing that confession was key to my forgiveness, both from God and from others.

God also began showing me that He did not want me to go and remind my abusers of their sins against me. Rather, my forgiveness had to be an act of pure love. Peter wrote, "Above all, love each other deeply, because love covers over a multitude of sins." (1 Peter 4:8) God's great love embraces and cherishes unworthy sinners.

I paused, praying that my heart would be so filled with God's love that there would be no room for unforgiveness, even though I had been hurt deeply. I asked the Lord to help me use whatever gifts I had received from Him to serve everyone as a faithful steward of God's grace in its various forms (1 Peter 4:10).

I then got to Luke 23:33-34. The scene was Christ's crucifixion. "When they came to the place called the Skull, they crucified him there, along with the criminals—one on his right, the other on his left. Jesus said, 'Father, forgive them, for they do not know what they are doing.'"

Goosebumps peppered my flesh. *Jesus asked His Father to forgive the people who orchestrated his death sentence? In the midst of His great pain and grief, Christ was courageous enough to ask His Father to forgive them? He was facing death, He knew what was ahead of Him, and even after He said what He said, they hurled more insults at Him.*

Still, he chose forgiveness anyway!

If Jesus was my greatest example, and if He was able to forgive others at the very point of His death on the cross, then I had to do the same—but the concept was so hard for me to accept. I always spoke of doing things the Jesus way. This *was* the Jesus way of forgiveness, but it was going to require an act of courage and a display of strength even in the midst of my deep hurt.

I needed to choose to forgive my captors, whether or not they knew what they were doing to me was sin. I had to replace the lie that my jailers had to know and acknowledge their sins before I forgave them and replace it with God's truth—the Jesus way—that they do not have to know or even repent.

I must forgive them anyway, and I cannot wait until I feel better to forgive. I thought. *I must forgive, if not for them, then for me.*

I was a follower of Jesus. That meant He was my leader. I read Hebrews 13:7-8, which summed it up. "Remember your leaders, who spoke the word of God to you. Consider the outcome of their way of life and imitate their faith. Jesus Christ is the same yesterday and today and forever."

As I chewed more on God's Word and consumed the many stories of Jesus that I knew so well, I again asked, *But where is the justice? What did Jesus, His disciples, and apostles like Paul, one of my heroes, think about justice?* It was not easy for me being at the receiving end of injustice and cruelty. I liked it when justice was done.

My mind then went to what Christ did when He carried His cross to Calvary's hill. I was thankful for what He did. His whole purpose was to save humanity from their burden of sins, one that was too heavy for anyone else but Him to bear. Still, somehow, Jesus found strength in the knowledge that our salvation from sin hinged on God's forgiveness.

So, where was justice? It clearly took so much love to bear the cruel injustices of others in the name of forgiveness. Surely it was painful. Christ must've gotten weary. He stumbled. He bled. But He made it to Calvary so we could be justified by faith in Him. As Romans 5 verses 1 and 9 proclaimed, "Therefore, since we have been justified through faith, we have peace with God through our Lord Jesus Christ ... Since we have now been justified by his blood, how much more shall we be saved from God's wrath through him!"

I realized that I was so wounded during my prison experiences that I struggled to forgive, and even when I said I did, I was basically pretending. But these verses revealed that Christ carried the burden of sinful humanity at His own demise, all in the name of seeking God's forgiveness for all of us.

I took an honest look at my need to truly and fully forgive those who had sinned against me while also genuinely recognizing my own sins. It helped me to fully understand that I had selfishly focused on forgiving my jailers *after* justice was done. I was pre-occupied by what I would do if my abusers did not acknowledge how they had hurt me or confess and repent of their wrongdoing against me. Since they were not believers in Christ, I also wondered how I would receive forgiveness from them if it was offered.

Yet Jesus was not concerned with what my heart and mind were preoccupied with. He simply required me to fully forgive, just as He did. I couldn't save them. Only Christ could do that. But I could forgive my offenders, and in doing so save myself from the emotional pain that was affecting how I interacted with and related to others.

I was starting to clearly see the path to healing, and it was paved with forgiveness.

I was starting to clearly see the path to healing, and it was paved with forgiveness.

As I continued to cry out in prayer and seek God's salvation from my distress, He took me to Psalm 107:20, which says of God, "He sent out his word and healed them; he rescued them from the grave." My hurt and pain, and the evil thoughts that were perpetuated by evil spirits, were stealing, destroying, and trying to kill my joy, purpose, health, visions, and dreams for my present and my future.

Jesus, however, wanted me to have life and have it abundantly (John 10:10). I needed to depend on Him as my healer. I knew Christ had healed many, cast out evil spirits, and set people free. I knew He was my source of strength and hope to live an abundant life. Even though I had continued to travel to many countries, I realized I had done so with a broken heart and wounds that still needed to be healed.

Psalm 147:3 told me that God "heals the brokenhearted and binds up their wounds." But I recognized that, even though I had experienced His deliverance and rescue from the hands of my jailers and the recovery of my wounded body, I still had unbelief and a lack of faith that He was able to heal my emotional pain. I needed to repent of my sin of doubt and depend upon His grace and mercy. I declared Psalm 41:4. "Have mercy on me, Lord; heal me, for I have sinned against you." I had to turn to God to take control over my heart, emotions, and mind, and bring healing and peace. I claimed the promise of Jeremiah 33:6. "I will bring health and healing to it; I will heal my people and will let them enjoy abundant peace and security."

While my physical injuries and scars, gruesome as they were, healed in their own timing, healing for my emotional and mental being—healing for my very soul—was not that easy for me. It was an unpleasant battle because I often had to remember those moments and relive the hurt. Anxiety and depression had kept me from sleeping normally for most of my life. But as I studied God's Word, I learned that as my soul healed, good health would follow (3 John 1:2), and that would allow my body to rest without nightmares and insomnia.

Just as I had many times before, I sought to be whole again—just as Jesus had healed others and made them whole. I understood that I could not face my jailers in my own strength. I prayed for strength and grace from God, and my study of forgiveness from His Word was giving me great hope and peace. It was also causing me to recognize that I lived in emotional extremes, one moment happy and singing, the next troubled and in need of help. I went back and forth like an emotional yo-yo, and most of the time, I was emotionally sick.

As I paused to pray for more strength from God, I remembered when Ezra said, "The joy of the Lord is your strength." (Nehemiah 8:10) He was speaking to the remnant of Israel who had returned to Jerusalem to rebuild the city and its temple. It was a time of restoration, not only of the ruined city, but also of obedience to the law of God. When the people heard Ezra declare the law, they wept in sorrow because they realized how far they had gone away from the Lord and His teaching. But Ezra told them to rejoice and celebrate because of the restoration that was taking place (Nehemiah 8:9-12).

It was my desire to be restored to good emotional health, rebuild my self-worth, and be completely healed, so I sought to start having the joy of the Lord. I thought back to the many times God had delivered me from prison and harm, and I allowed those remembrances to bring joy that could then give me the strength to face what was yet to come.

Then I read James 5:13-16. It declared, "Is anyone among you in trouble? Let them pray. Is anyone happy? Let them sing songs of praise. Is anyone among you sick? Let them call the elders of the church to pray over them and anoint them with oil in the name of the Lord. And the prayer offered in faith will make the sick person well; the Lord will raise them up. If they have sinned, they will be forgiven. Therefore, confess your sins to each other and pray for each other so that you may be healed. The prayer of a righteous person is powerful and effective."

I was convinced that if I met my abusers and practiced what this verse said to do, healing would come. My faith in God helped me feel at ease and gave me courage to forgive.

But will this verse work with those who are ungodly? I questioned myself fearfully. I prayed, "Dear Heavenly Father, I pray over my circumstances right now. I pray you will give me peace about what I can't change and the wisdom to change the things I can. I'm asking you to reach into my life and do your will. Guide me and give me the discernment to hear your voice. Help me to overcome these adversities and have victory in you on the other side when I visit those who hurt me, and even those I might have hurt along the way. Thank you for the plans you have for me, and I give you the praise and glory, even in this current storm and the ones yet to come. Save me from my distresses. Heal me completely and deliver me from destruction, and from the pain and hurt I carry. Release me from all of it."

I began to feel myself letting go of the intense emotional pain associated with my captors, and it was being replaced with inner resolution and peace. I started believing in the possibility of forgiving those who sinned against me, even when they remained unrepentant or had died since I last saw them. The idea of extending unrequested forgiveness empowered me and disarmed the power of sin. Even though I had not yet experienced reconciliation with my jailers, this deeper look into God's Word empowered me to move ahead. I felt freed to experience God's grace, healing, and joy in whole new way compared to the time I prayed with Dickson and the prayer warriors.

My prayer life also began to change. Ever since I had been kidnapped and tortured in northern Uganda, I had asked the Lord to never again allow evil circumstances to happen to me. I prayed for comfort and no persecution. I didn't want to get hurt again!

Of course, that wasn't what happened. Despite my requests to God, I had been imprisoned and abused on many more occasions. Now that I was understanding that I had no control over what evil people did to me, and that God sometimes allowed evil to happen for His good, my prayers were transformed.

"God, if or when I find myself in any situation, evil or good, may I be found faithful and trustworthy toward you and your Word," I prayed. "I give you glory in my suffering. Help me persevere and shape my character, that I will remember that my hope is in you. I give my life away so you can use me to your glory. I do not like to suffer, and I hate hardship, but I recognize that I am not in control. You are."

Slowly, I was growing more at peace as I read His Word, and hope began to build within me. Then I read the exhortation Paul gave in Romans 5:1-5. "Therefore, since we have been justified through faith, we have peace with God through our Lord Jesus Christ, through whom we have gained access by faith into this grace in which we now stand. And we boast in the hope of the glory of God. Not only so, but we also glory in our sufferings, because we know that suffering produces perseverance; perseverance, character; and character, hope. And hope does not put us to shame, because God's love has been poured out into our hearts through the Holy Spirit, who has been given to us."

To this day, it remains one of my favorite Bible passages. There *is* hope in every situation!

As I continued to study, I came to the place where Jesus healed the two blind men in Matthew 9:27-31, "Jesus warned them sternly, 'See that no one knows about this.' But they went out and spread the news about him all over that region." (verses 30-31) I heard the Holy Spirit leading me to be wiser as to what I communicated to those who sinned against me. I prayed that I would take the opportunity to spread the good news about Jesus like the two blind men did. They did not brag about their miraculous healing, but simply chose to tell others about Him.

Any healing I received was not for me to make known, but for the good news of Jesus to be known in all the places He was leading me to. God's Holy Spirit showed me that my healing would help others who were oppressed be free from anger, bitterness, rage, depression, and emotional pain.

Jesus was—and still is—in the business of forgiveness and healing. Jesus Christ "is the same yesterday and today and forever." (Hebrews 13:8)

That was just a fraction of what I studied, but I was healed more by what I learned about forgiveness during that two-week-long period than I was later when I actually went to forgive my captors and solidify the healing that I so greatly desired.

Even though I still felt unsettled, fearful, worried, and even depressed about meeting the jailers, I knew what I had to do. I sent a brief outline to my accountability partners and mission supporters, telling them that God was calling me to be obedient to find and forgive those who had offended me and to go back to the prisons where I was tortured.

I heard God say to me, "Be still, and know that I am God. I will be exalted among the nations. I will be exalted in the earth." I believed that God would be my fortress. I knew that I was a follower of Jesus and one of His sheep. I had to be obedient and follow the Lord wherever He led me (John 10:28). Jesus knew me, and that belief brought me more hope and courage.

I had also contacted Dr. Pede, a friend from Canada who came to Rochester from Calgary, Alberta and spent a week with me during my time of intensive prayer and study about forgiveness and healing. When we had first met years earlier, he was serving with World Medical Mission at Kapsowar Mission Hospital in western Kenya about 50 miles east of the border with Uganda. Dr. Pede was a Spirit-filled prayer warrior and minister, 70 years of age who, like the Apostle Paul, had chosen never to be married. He often joked with me that God's call upon me would match his if I, too, chose a life of celibacy.

We had an incredible time together studying more about forgiveness and healing as well as praying and worshipping. We often cried as we thought about God's grace and mercy. Some of Dr. Ben's friends and church leaders, two of whom were healing counselors, joined us as well. They were a big part of my healing process over those two weeks. I considered all of them to be the elders who are called upon to pray in James 5.

We read Proverbs 16:1-7 and laid out my plan before the Lord. We wanted it to be His plan, and we prayed that it would succeed in fulfilling its purpose of forgiveness, healing, and expanding the mission God had called me to do from the very beginning. God did not promise that all things would go my way, but I heard Him clearly promise that all things would work together for good as I trusted in Him.

I was also convinced that the Lord would cause my offenders to make peace with me as declared in Proverbs 16:7, and I found renewed faith from the Bible in Isaiah and Joshua. "So do not fear, for I am with you; do not be dismayed, for I am your God. I will strengthen you and help you; I will uphold you with my righteous right hand." (Isaiah 41:10) "Have I not commanded you? Be strong and courageous. Do not be afraid; do not be discouraged, for the Lord your God will be with you wherever you go." (Joshua 1:9) These words were like daily food, and I meditated upon them so that the lies of fear could be replaced with faith, courage, and hope.

Even with my plan in place, I still had ups and downs thinking about what was to come. I didn't handle the uncertainty gracefully, but I knew I needed to keep moving and honoring the vision the Lord had given me, even if others thought I shouldn't after all of my earlier imprisonments and abuse. It was overwhelming at times to consider returning to all of those places—but God showed me that this process of forgiveness was going to take time. It wasn't going to be a quick fix. It wasn't going to be as simple as meeting, saying a short statement, and leaving. I chose to believe that I was on God's path despite floods of doubt and fear, and even if I didn't understand how He was going to open all the doors for me to return to all of the places where I had been hurt.

God showed me that this process of forgiveness was going to take time.

One thing was for certain, though. I wasn't going to return to northern Uganda to meet with any of my abductors from the Lord's Resistance Army. All these years later, their rebel leaders are believed to have gone into hiding in the Congo or southern Sudan if they aren't still in Uganda. In my pride and self-righteousness, a part of me badly wanted to loudly tell them how gracious it was for me to forgive them even though they hadn't asked for it. I wanted them to feel guilt and shame.

But God, in His grace, convicted me of my arrogance. I took great comfort in knowing I wasn't going to try to find them, but that I would forgive them anyway. God assured me that forgiveness was not the same as reconciliation, and that He honored the desire of my heart to forgive them without having to meet them.

Forgiveness was my choice—and forgiving the LRA was for me and my benefit.

As I thought further about what I was about to do, I had to acknowledge and embrace that I could again be thrown into prison and abused. My forgiveness of my captors was not going to be based on their actions. It was my responsibility, and that was a real leap of faith for me. I also had to accept that while I wanted to hold my offenders accountable for their sins against me, justice was up to God, not me. I didn't want to let them off the hook, but I had to let God speak into their hearts and execute justice for me (Romans 12:19-21; 1 Peter 2:21-23). My only role was to forgive.

Because most of the jailers were unreliable and mean spirited, I realized my words and my response to them had to come from the Lord. I did pray for God to change their hearts even before I met with them, and the Holy Spirit also led me to pray for my own attitude and actions when I saw them again. My victim mindset made that very hard to do, but the Lord helped me.

In the end, the thought of going back was unpleasant because I was terrified, but I saw God, in His sovereignty, had already known in advance that I would someday be returning to them to offer forgiveness. Knowing that this process was for my good, and that He was going to use it for His glory, began to relieve my emotional pain.

Memories of my past abuse still triggered me to relive them as though they were happening again, but I pressed on, subjecting that trauma to the authority of God. I prayed for the Lord to work in my mind just as He had with Paul when he wrote, "We demolish arguments and every pretension that sets itself up against the knowledge of God, and we take captive every thought to make it obedient to Christ." (2 Corinthians 10:5)

After my memorable stay in New York, I returned to Northern Ireland for a couple of weeks, and then back to Kenya to visit my family for a week, before beginning the journeys to visit my past captors. On my way back to Belfast from New York, I thought of God's goodness to make sure I had taken that month-plus of rest, and I reflected about how His divine healing was for me and for everyone. I had gone through so much suffering and hurt.

Why hadn't I taken time to allow myself to heal sooner? I had seen Jesus heal so many individuals and seen how even evil spirits were cast out of people, such as Ibrahim's son. I knew from God's Word how others were touched and delivered by the Lord when they had faith in Him. Mark 5:34 says that "Jesus went through all the towns and villages, teaching in their synagogues, proclaiming the good news of the kingdom and healing every disease and sickness." In Matthew 9:35, Jesus spoke to the woman who dared to touch the hem of His garment. "He said to her, 'Daughter, your faith has healed you. Go in peace and be freed from your suffering.'" In Mark 10:52, we read that the Lord said to the blind man, "'Go,' said Jesus, 'your faith has healed you.'" Immediately he received his sight and followed Jesus along the road."

It was because of their faith that they were healed. Why was it that I had read and preached from all those scriptures and seen many people healed, yet struggled with my own emotional and mental sickness?

The week after I returned to Belfast, I began studying from two Bibles given to me by one of Dr. Ben's pastors. One was the Amplified Version of the Scriptures; the other, which I read the most, was the New King James Version. I learned about the many barriers that had hindered my healing and freedom. These were things I had noticed in others, but not in myself. It hurt to admit that I had prayed for many to believe in God and receive their healing, but had failed to intentionally do the same thing for myself in my deepest spiritual, emotional, and mental being.

The first barrier I recognized was my *pride*. I had avoided asking for help. I didn't want to take actions to change my situation or seek the solution to my abuse. My victim mindset only increased that pride. Yet James 4:6 says of the Lord, "But He gives more grace. Therefore, He says: 'God resists the proud, but gives grace to the humble.'" (NKJV) Isaiah 57:15 added, "For thus says the High and Lofty One Who inhabits eternity, whose name is Holy: 'I dwell in the high and holy place, With him who has a contrite and humble spirit, to revive the spirit of the humble, And to revive the heart of the contrite ones.'" (NKJV) I saw that I needed to learn how to have humility in my situation, and that was difficult for me. Our circumstances and our suffering can humble us to receive what God has in store for us. I still struggle with pride from time to time, and I don't ask for help like I should when I am in need. I fear negative responses from others.

As I mediated and prayed about my barriers to healing, I read Romans 10:17. It teaches that "faith comes by hearing, and hearing by the word of God." (NKJV) Isaiah 5:13 says, "Therefore my people have gone into captivity, Because they have no knowledge." (NKJV) I understood that knowledge of God's Word builds faith—including faith in Him as a healer. Jesus constantly told people, "Your faith has healed you" or "by faith you are healed," yet I had not applied that to my situation. Therefore, I saw that *ignorance of the Word of God* had hindered me from receiving the truth I needed to replace the lies that claimed God was not able to heal me. I had read God's Word, but I still allowed many doubts and questions to be a barrier to my faith.

I came to Mark 6:5-6 and read, "Now He could do no mighty work there, except that He laid His hands on a few sick people and healed them. And He marveled because of their unbelief." (NKJV) That was me—and it revealed another barrier: my *unbelieving spirit*. It had prevented me from going into God's promises and believing that He could heal me. I had seen God deliver me from prisons and heal me physically, but I had not believed that He could restore my emotional and mental issues. I had to truly have faith that nothing is impossible for God. Hebrew 3:12-13 declares, "Beware, brethren, lest there be in any of you an evil heart of unbelief in departing from the living God; but exhort one another daily, while it is called 'Today,' lest any of you be hardened through the deceitfulness of sin." (NKJV)

As I reflected again about my mindset that those who had done bad things to me should also suffer the way I had suffered, I was convicted of those sinful thoughts and had to repent of my deceitfulness. This led me to recognize the next barrier to my healing: bitterness and anger that led to *unforgiveness*. I affirmed that I needed to forgive first, knowing that the emotion from that act would follow. Mark 11:25-26 teaches, "And whenever you stand praying, if you have anything against anyone, forgive him, that your Father in heaven may also forgive you your trespasses. But if you do not forgive, neither will your Father in heaven forgive your trespasses." (NKJV) Unforgiveness was hindering me from receiving the healing power of God I needed for my hurting heart.

As I received revelation through my study of forgiveness and healing, it was also affirmed that I needed to deal with my *unconfessed sin*, not the sins of the people who had hurt me. In Psalm 32:3-5, David said, "When I kept silent, my bones grew old Through my groaning all the day long. For day and night Your hand was heavy upon me; My vitality was turned into the drought of summer. Selah. I acknowledged my sin to You, And my iniquity I have not hidden. I said, 'I will confess my transgressions to the Lord,' and You forgave the iniquity of my sin. Selah." (NKJV) I knew I had to confess my prideful sins.

Through my emotional pain, anxiety, anger, bitterness, depression, and even suicidal thoughts, I had an all-around negative attitude. I had told myself and others that I would never heal. Even as I was traveling and ministering to others, I had decided that healing wasn't going to happen to me, so I kept on doing what I was doing, hoping to either die or that Christ would come. I'd tell myself things like, "I am not worthy of life here" or "I am ugly and shameful." That made me hopeless.

Yet what I said about myself and others was important. I realized that my *negative confessions* had hindered the healing process each time I was hurt. I had to renounce all negative thinking and confession, and believe what Paul wrote in Philippians 4:8. "Finally, brethren, whatever things are true, whatever things are noble, whatever things are just, whatever things are pure, whatever things are lovely, whatever things are of good report, if there is any virtue and if there is anything praiseworthy—meditate on these things." (NKJV)

I know it is not easy to think of these things or embrace these godly and powerful words when we are in pain or feel bitter, angry, lonely, hurting, and depressed. But the truth is it works—and when I apply them, hold myself accountable, and believe, I can then take action. Speaking and professing life, and the renewed attitude that brings, makes healing real to me. I have learned that I will eventually end up doing whatever I continuously think about. As Proverbs 23:7 teaches of humanity, "For as he thinks in his heart, so *is* he." (NKJV)

Thanks to Paul's words in Philippians 4, I am committed and pray to have eyes that see the best in people, a heart that forgives the worst, a mind that forgets the bad, and a soul that never loses faith in God, even during the toughest times.

As I continued to process what had happened with me, I recognized that I *lacked persistence* in seeking God's help in prayer—and that it had hindered my healing. In Luke 18:1-8, Jesus shares the parable of the persistent widow. He began by saying that we should always pray and not lose heart. The parable is about a widow who repeatedly goes to a judge to make her case. Even though he doesn't respect her or God, he gives in to her because of her persistence. If the evil judge was moved by her persistence, how much more so is God moved by our persistence? Jesus then asked, "When the Son of Man comes, will He really find faith on the earth?" (verse 8)

Christ desires us to have persistent faith. I saw that when I was wounded, my faith had melted. I hadn't prayed or sought God's healing until it became worse and worse. Yet Jesus said in Matthew 7:7-8 "Ask, and it will be given to you; seek, and you will find; knock, and it will be opened to you. For everyone who asks receives, and he who seeks finds, and to him who knocks it will be opened." (NKJV) I needed to learn to constantly seek my healing and pray for God to change my situation. I had to keep crying out to the Lord in my pain.

In the Bible, I discovered in Luke 1 how Zacharias and his wife had prayed persistently to have a child, and when they were well past the age of childbearing, the angel brought the news that they were going to have a son. He became John the Baptist. In Luke 2:36-39, I read about an amazing woman named Anna. She was a prophetess who, at the age of 84, persistently prayed night and day for the redemption of Jerusalem.

I couldn't help but sometimes wonder if God didn't hear me or if He was holding out on me just to make things challenging, but Daniel prayed and fasted for 21 days before he saw a breakthrough. That story is in Daniel 10, and Daniel learned that his words had been heard from the very first day he began praying, but the answer had been delayed because of spiritual warfare (Daniel 10:12-14). If we don't see a change when we pray, that doesn't mean our words were not heard. There is a spiritual battle going on all the time, so we must be persistent instead of preoccupied by our own self-pity.

On the other hand, while I knew that God had allowed me to experience everything I'd been through, my experiences were not like the one Paul talked about in 2 Corinthians 12:8-10. He revealed, "Concerning this thing I pleaded with the Lord three times that it might depart from me. And He said to me, 'My grace is sufficient for you, for My strength is made perfect in weakness.' Therefore, most gladly I will rather boast in my infirmities, that the power of Christ may rest upon me. Therefore, I take pleasure in infirmities, in reproaches, in needs, in persecutions, in distresses, for Christ's sake. For when I am weak, then I am strong." (NKJV)

I desperately wanted my pain and suffering to go away, so I did not approach it like Paul did. But I'd come to embrace Paul's words as I continued to serve when I went to visit the jailers and those who had hurt me the most.

In my victim mindset, I had justified some of my behaviors and allowed myself to make excuses, become defensive, or try to cover up my faults and failures. But I knew I needed to learn to do the right thing to change my situation and heal. The words from Romans 7:21-24 had become my way of life: When I want to do what is right, I always do what is wrong. While my mind and heart agree with the law of God, there is a different law at work deep inside of me that fights with my mind. That law of sin holds me in its power because sin is still in me; therefore, I am not happy. Who can set me free from my sinful self? Thank God, I can be free through Jesus Christ my Lord!

The answer is Jesus! Our freedom, understanding, and power to change our situation is in Him. We need to trust Him and allow Him to work in our hearts because sin causes pain in our lives and in the lives of others.

Because of the lessons learned about the hindrances to my healing, I experienced a release of resentment, anger, bitterness, and even hate. It was vitally important for my mental health as a victim of abuse. It propelled me forward rather than keeping me emotionally engaged in the injustice of my trauma. Forgiveness elevated my mood, infused my optimism, and guarded against stress, anxiety, and depression. By forgiving, I let go of my grievances and judgments and allowed myself to heal. It was a total rebuild and restoration of who I was.

By forgiving, I let go of my grievances and judgments and allowed myself to heal.

It wasn't easy, and it still sometimes feels impossible, but it's achievable as we believe His truth instead of lies. I replaced the lies that God would not be able to heal me or to prevent my persecution and suffering from happening again with the knowledge of His *truth* so I would know and have a greater understanding of His ways. I reminded myself that prayers may not prevent bad situations from happening, but I still needed to pray for change to take place within me during evil circumstances, trusting in God and in what He can do. God is our healer and deliverer in times of trouble.

I'll always remember the feeling of having a heavy weight lifted off of me when I truly forgave. I developed a new attitude and self-belief that motivated me to take action, obey God, and go meet my captors. Unforgiveness had been holding me back from my future and the plans God had for me. I was stuck asking "why" instead of trusting the Lord and His Word. Unforgiveness had caused resentment, bitterness, anger, fear, hostility, and hatred in my heart. It had affected every relationship I had with men, women, the people I served, authorities and church leaders, and even God. Before forgiving the hurt, I would have to admit that I was filled with thoughts of retribution or revenge. I didn't know how to resolve the situations, and though I knew I was still human, I was sometimes even addicted to the adrenaline that anger, hate, and revenge provided.

I worked hard to minimize my pain. I tried to stuff it away, but it was hard to forget the hurt, and I could not wish away the memories. Yet now I have learned that memories cannot be healed, but our emotions, mental health, and even spiritual well-being can be. I have heard the saying "forgive and forget," and while I find that forgiveness is very possible, forgetting is impossible. Memories of the past do not just go away even after forgiveness and healing is achieved—but it's what I do with my memories that determine my present and my future spiritual well-being. Therefore, I do not want to relapse into anger and bitterness because that causes me to look backward.

I am not perfect, even after God's healing in my life. I can still find myself living in a rut, focusing on hurtful thoughts and feelings of helplessness, fear, and loneliness. I know that I have to constantly remain focused on God and His truth. Still, experiencing forgiveness has unlocked how my past is no longer controlling my present, and my future has hope. I have learned to face each day with courage, excitement, and joy, even in times of uncertainty about what the future may bring.

So, as I prepared to meet my captors, I wasn't bold, but I was ready to do it. I wasn't going back for the purpose of reconciling relationships. I did not plan to have a relationship or friendship with them, even though God certainly had His plans. I did not expect my abusers to accept or reject me, but I decided to be ready for anything and hold on to the hope of God's promise in Joshua 1:9. "Have I not commanded you? Be strong and courageous. Do not be afraid; do not be discouraged, for the Lord your God will be with you wherever you go."

All I knew was that my return was not going to be a mission of retaliation. Instead, I was anxious to see what God was going to do since He promised to be with me. I kept reminding myself He had delivered me many times before, and I knew He was going to have His way.

Though God had given me forgiveness and healing, that didn't mean that I felt good about the situation and that everything was going to be okay with me when I met them. I did not have to forget the evil incidences as if they never happened. Again, forgiving them was for *me*. I wanted them to know that I was accepting the reality of what happened and gracefully living in a state of resolution with it. As I did this, I hoped they would see Jesus in me and be drawn to Him.

The battle in my mind and my heart was real and terrifying. What if they were not there when I arrived? How will I even find my way to meet with them? How will I even begin to have a conversation with them if I do meet them?

A friend of mine once told me, "Any transition, temptation, and trouble always creates questions," and that had certainly proven to be true in my experiences. This was a transition, and it was troubling to be uncertain about what was yet to come. Proverbs 18:21 declares, "The tongue has the power of life and death, and those who love it will eat its fruit." I understood from that verse that every word I chose to say when I met my captors would either bring life or death.

The stakes were high. My word would build up others or tear them down. They would give hope, love, peace, unity, correction, healing, knowledge, and wisdom, or they would cause anger, hate, bitterness, jealousy, contempt, violence, judgment, condemnation, and confusion. In the end, it was my choice. My words would bear fruit, and that reminded me of Galatians 5:22-23. "But the fruit of the Spirit is love, joy, peace, forbearance, kindness, goodness, faithfulness, gentleness and self-control. Against such things there is no law."

Those were the fruits I so desperately needed going forward.

God did not give me a spirit of fear, but of power, love, and self-discipline (2 Timothy 1:7). Only through God and the power of His Holy Spirit would I be able to achieve all of these as I readied myself to set off on my journey to visit and forgive those who had hurt me so deeply.

Chapter 9

FORGIVENESS REALIZED

I procrastinated as long as I could, and I was reluctant to pray about my return. It made me feel helpless, depressed, and frustrated. I was very uncomfortable and felt even more pain at just the thought of meeting my persecutors.

There was nothing fun about God's command to go and forgive them, but I did know that when the Lord spoke and led the way, He must have a plan, even if I did not understand it.

Even in my fear and doubt, there was a glimpse of hope—knowing that God had gotten me out of prisons before and He'd probably do it again if I was taken captive.

God wanted me to face my challenges rather than look for an easy way out. I didn't want to go and see them again face to face. It was challenging enough figuring out how and where I was going to have the meetings. While I did have contact with some of the "men of peace" who had earlier betrayed me to the authorities, I did not have contact with any of those authorities or my captors. I only recalled images of some of the police stations where I was interrogated, the prisons where I was incarcerated, or of the captors themselves. I did not know any of them.

The first people I talked to about my plans, about seven friends in all, responded negatively. They feared I'd end up in prison once more, and they didn't believe in me or God's vision any longer.

One of them quoted Proverbs 12:15 to me, saying, "The way of fools seems right to them, but the wise listen to advice." This discouraged me, and I wondered if perhaps God was speaking through them that I shouldn't go. That caused me to question myself further and doubt the Lord. Another friend insisted, "You went before and were imprisoned. Evil things happened to you. What makes you think it will be any different this time?"

Those questions made me angrier and more anxious, and a great battle waged within me between what they were saying and what I believed God had told me to do.

Yet the Lord's voice kept ringing in my heart. *You will return to those places.* I was conflicted and struggled emotionally, spiritually, and mentally; however, I knew being obedient to God's voice was the right thing to do.

Trusting that God had my future in the palm of His hand, I refused to focus on the past, worked to shake off my present hang ups, and sought to have faith in Him to give me the ability to face the future. I received hope from Romans 15:13. It declared, "May the God of hope fill you with all joy and peace as you trust in him, so that you may overflow with hope by the power of the Holy Spirit."

I couldn't do this on my own. I needed the strength of the Holy Spirit. I felt a powerful shift within me that built my faith and tore down the negative thoughts from the past. Only God could do that, and He was—and still is—the foundation I need to build up and solidify my heart and my mind.

I then reached out to a couple of my close friends and to my accountability team, all of whom were supportive, and they encouraged me to find someone to travel with me. At first, I couldn't think of anyone who would agree to do that, but I called

Ibrahim in Morocco. I shared everything the Lord had told me to do, and I asked for his opinion, fully intending to ask him to go with me. I wasn't sure exactly how I was going to do that, even after he had traveled with me previously, but I was determined.

Ibrahim said, "There is nothing you cannot do when God is leading you. Listen to Him and to what He is speaking to you."

Instantly, I felt the affirmation and confirmation I'd been hoping for. We talked for a long time before I finally said, "I feel God is telling me that you should go with me where you can." I gave him many reasons to agree, including to facilitate peaceful meetings with the "men of peace" and the captors, and to help me with language barriers.

I knew it was a lot to ask of Ibrahim.

"I will sit on it," he said, "and we will talk within the next few days."

When he got back to me, Ibrahim agreed to arrange for my meeting of the captors in Morocco and to travel with me to Mauritania and Yemen. Due to his personal commitments, he suggested we travel to those places one after another, which was not ideal because I wasn't sure I'd have energy for it. I also didn't know if I'd even make it out of the first meeting with my captors.

Still, it was such a relief to know that Ibrahim was going to be with me. We'd be going two-by-two, just like Jesus sent out His disciples. It was also an honor to have Ibrahim travel with me. I enjoyed his company, and he said he was most excited about learning Scripture together as we went from place to place.

We'd always done that before, picking out a book of the Bible from which to study. However, I wasn't thinking about that at all for this trip. I was too focused on the task at hand.

Then Ibrahim added another request. "My son, Rahman, would like to join us and spend time with you."

I had briefly met Rahman back when I first visited Ibrahim,

when Rahman's brother was delivered, but I had not interacted with him. Since then, Ibrahim told me, Rahman had accepted the Lord and was excited to come with us. "You need to pick a book from the Bible that all three of us can study as we travel," Ibrahim said.

I became concerned. *Ibrahim does not have the same fears and doubts I do. Our goals for this trip do not appear to be lining up.* "How about we talk about this later when I get to Morocco?" I asked.

"We cannot wait until then. My son needs to book his tickets to accompany us," Ibrahim explained. That made sense to me, so I agreed to his request, as long as he picked the Bible book. Ibrahim chose Proverbs, and he committed to take care of all the expenses for the three of us to travel to the three countries. That was a huge gift because I didn't have enough financial support to cover the trip. Everything was set.

I arrived in Morocco with no difficulty at immigration. My plan was to spend a few days with Ibrahim and his family. I wanted to make sure he fully understood why I was going to meet my captors. As we talked the night I arrived, Ibrahim read Luke 6:31— "Do to others as you would have them do to you"—and then asked me what I thought.

"Those are words of wisdom," I responded.

He smiled. "When I introduce you to your captors, I will quote this scripture and tell them you have come to do what they did to you."

I love to laugh, and Ibrahim certainly had a sense of humor. But I couldn't help but be a little unsettled at the thought of him actually saying that.

The next day I decided to spend time with Rahman since he was staying at their home. I wanted to get to know more about him as well as some of his other brothers and family, including Razik, the brother who had been delivered. I also desired to lay low and not get involved in anything that would cause any trouble.

That afternoon, Ibrahim said some of his family members wanted to be baptized. I was concerned that might again draw the attention of the authorities, but Ibrahim arranged to fill their animal trough with water and allow me to do the baptisms there at his home.

In all, five members of Ibrahim's family were baptized. As they were being baptized, a cigar-smoking gentleman named Karim watched. He asked if he, too, could be baptized, but when I went to dunk him into the trough, he said he wanted to keep his cigar in his mouth.

I'd never seen anything like it, and I told him the water would put it out. "The water will surrender the cigar's flame!" I kidded.

But he didn't care. It's funny and amazing how God works!

When Karim came out of the water, soggy stogie still between his lips, I asked him how he felt.

He grabbed the dripping cigar so he could respond. "I feel great," he exclaimed, "but I didn't understand what you meant by, 'I baptize you in the name of the Father, the Son, and the Holy Spirit.'"

Ibrahim and I ended up spending the entire night with Karim, Rahman, Razik, and a few other men talking about faith in God, being a disciple of Jesus, and comparing the teachings of the Quran and the Bible. Ibrahim would continue discipling

It's funny and amazing how God works!

Karim—and today he is busy making disciples in Northern Africa. I have enjoyed serving alongside Karim. He has faced persecution as a follower of Jesus, but God has continued to be gracious to him, and it has been an honor to minister with him.

Karim no longer smokes cigars—and since then, neither he nor I have ever baptized anyone smoking one.

The next afternoon, Ibrahim, Rahman, and I went to the police station where I had been interrogated. It was daunting. I was scared, and my heart was racing. Not only was I facing the fear and uncertainty of seeing my captors again, but I was afraid that news of the previous day's baptisms had somehow reached the authorities there. I wondered if I was walking into the lion's den.

The chief of police came out to meet us, and thankfully, Ibrahim did not quote Luke 6:31. Instead, he and the police chief excused themselves and left the room.

I did not recognize the police chief, but their departure only made me more anxious. Rahman and I stayed in the office, and as we waited, he wanted to engage me in conversation about God and the Bible. Honestly, at that moment, I wished he'd just be quiet. Nothing he was asking had anything to do with why I was there. But, out of respect, I didn't want to tell Rahman to just leave me alone.

Rahman had a notebook with him. He opened it and pointed to one of the pages.

"Can you explain here what you wrote to my dad months ago?"

"Sure," I said tensely, "and make it the last question until we leave the police station, please."

Then he read, "Rejoice in the Lord always. I will say it again: Rejoice! Let your gentleness be evident to all. The Lord is near. Do not be anxious about anything, but in every situation, by prayer and petition, with thanksgiving, present your requests to God. And the peace of God, which transcends all understanding, will guard your hearts and your minds in Christ Jesus."

He sat in silence, awaiting my explanation.

"What is the reference on your note?" I asked.

"There is no reference. I wrote that, but I have no idea what you are asking," Rahman responded, confused.

"That is from the Apostle Paul in Philippians 4:4-7," I said.

"I see your life on this note," Rahman told me. "You rejoice and pray a lot. God's peace is in you, so I wanted to understand what this means."

Without another word, I fell on my knees in tears, right there in the office of the police chief. Overwhelmed by emotion, I realized I was being the exact opposite of what Paul said in that passage.

God has a way of ministering to me when I am at my weakest: anxious with no peace of mind and no joy. The Lord used Rahman, who was simply seeking to understand that passage for himself.

Moments later, Ibrahim and the police chief returned, along with three other police officers. I was still down on my knees, quietly praying for God to remove my anxiety and for His peace to guard my heart and mind. As awkward as it was, I embraced the moment. I got up and sat back on the seat, filled with peace and courage.

"Are you okay?" Ibrahim asked in dismay.

"Yes, I am!" I declared. "I was just having a moment with the Lord."

I was then told that two of the officers were the ones who had ordered my arrest, but I could sense that the atmosphere in the room was not as tense as it was the first time when I was interrogated.

"We have heard that Allah sent you to speak to us," the police chief said.

"Sir, I assume your statement is based on your consultation with Ibrahim," I replied, "and, yes, by His grace, He has preserved my life to see this day. I am already blessed to be in your office right now in this manner. It is different from when I was at this station in the past."

"What do you want us to do?" the police chief asked. His question caused me to panic.

"Sir, all I have is love. I am a follower of Jesus, and in Him I have peace because of the forgiveness of my sins when He died on the cross for me. That forgiveness is something I am working on even as I serve Him. When I was in this place before, I was found guilty of breaking the law of the land, even though it was God showing love for His people that led to Ibrahim's son being healed when he believed in God and was restored."

I concluded, "Despite it all, I was freed, and so I came just to appreciate you. That's what God is leading me to say here."

It was uncomfortable looking at the unfriendly faces of the officers, but I remembered Paul's wise words from Colossians 4:5-6. "Be wise in the way you act toward outsiders; make the most of every opportunity. Let your conversation be always full of grace, seasoned with salt, so that you may know how to answer everyone." Clearly, the officers were outsiders to my faith. I needed my conversation to be both so that they didn't hear any condemnation from what I was saying to them.

I continued. "When in prison here, I was hurting. When I left, I was wounded. Over time, God restored me. I acknowledge my wrong. I was prideful and arrogant when I was arrested, and I was ignorant about how disrespectful I was to the law. Today, I came to be a messenger of love and forgiveness. I ask for forgiveness on my part and for my God to have mercy on me. I am here in obedience to the teachings of the Holy Scripture, the Bible, and Jesus Christ my Savior. As you had said earlier, Allah sent me to speak those words to you. I have also read in your holy book, the Quran, the passage that says to adopt forgiveness, instruct what is right, and ignore the foolish. For that reason, I asked my brother, Ibrahim, to bring me here. Thank you."

The police chief rose from his seat, came over to me, kissed me on both of my cheeks, and gave me a hug. The other officers did the same thing.

With great emotion in his voice, the police chief responded, "Thank you for your courage and your love. You are our brother. God's love and peace is in you. May Allah have mercy. Our job was to ensure law and order. Is there anything we can do for you?"

With tears in my eyes, I replied, "Thank you for your welcome and for this opportunity to meet you." I then requested to be allowed to visit the prison and the prison wardens who tortured me, but that request was declined due to what they identified as security and privacy issues.

There were more hugs and kisses. I had never felt such relief. It was as though a huge weight dropped from my shoulders. I was greatly content with that short conversation, and I could not stop thanking God as we were escorted to the entrance gate.

Just as we were saying goodbye, the police chief invited me to visit his home before I left the country. Totally unexpected, I instantly agreed to do it.

I began seeing the benefit of embracing forgiveness. The police chief and his officers did not literally say, "Please forgive us for our sin and wrongdoing," but I felt their genuine remorse, especially after receiving that invitation.

I left the police station different than when I first arrived fearful and scared. More than that, the way God ministered to me through Rahman was better than I could have ever imagined. Rahman and I continued our discussion after departing from the station. He was a true seeker of God's truth, and today he disciples many who are involved in house church multiplication efforts.

I began seeing the benefit of embracing forgiveness.

Two days later, Ibrahim took me to the police chief's home where we enjoyed a sweet reception dinner. There were a few other guests invited, and there were more conversations about faith and questions about the ministry. The police chief also arranged to have two of the prison wardens who tortured me join us for dinner—and it was there that both of them asked me to forgive them. I wept.

The police chief then asked me to pray for them and over them. Ibrahim and I did so, and we continued to minister to them until we left just before 11:00 p.m. That evening was truly one of a kind!

The police chief has since retired, but he is my friend to this day. I still visit him when I can, and he remains a Muslim. Some of the other guests at that dinner, however, have become followers of Christ. God's way is amazing! That dinner was the last time I saw the prison wardens, but before I left Morocco, I was taken to visit the prison where I was previously detained, though I was not allowed to go inside.

All of it was beyond my expectations. I saw how God continued to use Ibrahim as a man of peace and with his influence to help me through the journey and ministry.

I was exhausted and needed to rest after going to the prison. I remained with Ibrahim's family and friends, and we started reading the book of Proverbs together. So many verses were profound to us, such as Proverbs 3:5-6, which declares, "Trust in the Lord with all your heart and lean not on your own understanding; in all your ways submit to him, and he will make your paths straight." I knew I needed to trust the Lord more as Ibrahim, Rahman, and I debriefed each other on our time in Morocco and reflected on our next move.

After six days in Morocco, we flew to Nouakchott, the capital of Mauritania, in hopes of meeting the "men of peace" and visiting the prison there. We landed, I didn't have issues with immigration or customs, and we went directly to the hotel we had booked for the next four days.

Upon our arrival there, I again became stressed. It was my first visit to Mauritania after being released from prison and told to never come back. Memories of the torture returned, including abuse at the police station where I was interrogated, urinated upon, and had a truncheon shoved into my rear end, and it made me hesitant to go back to that place. Ibrahim and his son left me at the hotel so they could meet with his friends, one of whom was the Islamic preacher who had done such evil to me during my last visit.

After our morning devotion through Proverbs 12, Ibrahim warned me to be careful, reminding me that Mauritania was a different country than Morocco, and with very different people. Our meeting with the Islamic preacher was going to be that afternoon by the mosque where he preached. He was also a government official and well respected regarding his business influences. After that meeting, we were then going to have dinner with some of Ibrahim's friends.

I remained very uncertain and uneasy about being in Mauritania due to its extreme intolerance toward people who believed in something other than Islam. I had such a heavy heart that I decided to spend time alone to pray and try to relax. The Holy Spirit led me to Isaiah 43:2, which says, "When you pass through the waters, I will be with you; and when you pass through the rivers, they will not sweep over you. When you walk through the fire, you will not be burned; the flames will not set you ablaze." I sensed the scripture was revealing what I might have to walk through that afternoon, and it was giving me the assurance of God's protection. I remembered how Jesus comforted His disciples in John 14:1. He told them, "Do not let your hearts be troubled. You believe in God; believe also in me."

I needed to believe in Jesus and God.

When we arrived at the meeting place, the Islamic preacher and his team of five other men were there. It was a cold welcome compared to when I'd first met him. At the beginning, he conversed mainly with Ibrahim and his friends. Then he turned to me and was quite direct.

"You came here to Nouakchott working with illegal groups, inciting rebellion, calling us slave masters, and disrespecting our country and culture. You were spreading false religion and blaspheming Islam. You deserved your punishment under the law."

I felt gutted at his words, harsh tone, and demeanor. It was tense, and I was scared. I could easily see myself being taken to prison once again.

Ibrahim then spoke with the preacher and his team. I had no idea what they were saying because they communicated in French. I had very little understanding of that language. As I observed, I could see that Ibrahim was gentle, compassionate, and appeared to be persuasive. The conversation went on for about 10 minutes, with Ibrahim briefly turning to me to explain that he was telling them what I had gone through.

Moments later, Ibrahim asked me if I would like to say anything.

Nervously, I replied, "I recognize my wrong in breaking the law. It was not my intention, and it was not my plan when I came here. Please forgive me for whatever wrong I did in your eyes."

The Islamic preacher said, "Since you admit you blaspheme and were wrong, you should be punished more now!"

I began to panic, knowing full well the painful prison experience I'd already had there in Mauritania. I tried to hold my voice steady as I spoke. "The peace of God filled my heart, and I was healed. I asked Ibrahim to bring me here so I could testify that God forgave my sin while I was yet a sinner. His love for me is what influenced me to return."

I took a breath as the preacher responded.

"When you leave, do not return here again. Out of respect for our brother, Ibrahim, we will let you go."

That was it. The meeting was over.

No one shook hands. There was no remorse or any apologetic feeling from them whatsoever.

I was relieved that I was not going to be imprisoned or punished, but I remained unsettled as we left. As we had read that morning from Proverbs 12:6 and 18: "The words of the wicked lie in wait for blood, but the speech of the upright rescues them … The words of the reckless pierce like swords, but the tongue of the wise brings healing." I pondered those verses as we drove to get dinner.

I was cautious not to say or do anything that could get me into trouble, as though there were spies all around us. Ibrahim and Rahman did most of the talking as we ate, and they mostly spoke in French. I was asked to pray at the end of the meal before we left for the hotel.

While I had wanted to find out about the prison where I was first detained, I knew it was wise not to ask. I would not have recognized it anyway since I was blindfolded most of the time I was incarcerated. But Ibrahim and Rahman later revealed that they found out I had been interrogated at Tevragh Zeina police station and had been held at Dar Naim Prison.

I stayed in my hotel room the rest of the time we were in Mauritania. That provided much needed rest and time for reflection and meditation. During that time, God showed me that freedom comes when I learn how to let go by refusing to entertain fear and by releasing those who had hurt me. Romans 12:17-19 says, "Do not repay anyone evil for evil. Be careful to do what is right in the eyes of everyone. If it is possible, as far as it depends on you, live at peace with everyone. Do not take revenge, my dear friends, but leave room for God's wrath, for it is written: 'It is mine to avenge; I will repay,' says the Lord."

I was glad that I could leave at peace, even as I came to terms with the fact that I could not change the evils that had happened to me or change the hearts of the people who had hurt me. I *could* change myself, my attitude, and my heart, and view the bad experiences as opportunities for God to manifest Himself and for me to recognize His ways through them.

Then, at midnight of our last day in Mauritania, three of the Islamic preacher's team members came to our hotel. I was deeply terrified, thinking I was going to be arrested—only to learn that they had come to ask questions about following the teachings of Jesus!

Ibrahim and I led them to a prayer of confession as they committed themselves to be Christ followers. They left the hotel around 4:00 a.m., and when we arrived at the airport that afternoon to catch our flight to Casablanca, Morocco, all three of them were at the airport with their families to see us off.

God's purposes and ways are beyond my knowledge! Even though one of those individuals has since died, their families are still underground believers, and I was honored to visit with them in 2009 as we were training oral Bible storytelling as a tool for discipleship. Today, Mauritania remains a challenging place to do Christian mission work.

We returned to Morocco, and I decided to stay there for four days until Ibrahim, Rahman, and I left for Yemen and its capital city of Sana'a. The three of us had finished reading and discussing the book of Proverbs, and I learned much reading Proverbs with my fellow disciples. I could not imagine facing the recent challenges without them.

We decided to continue studying the Bible as the Holy Spirit led us, particularly regarding the subject of the persecution of believers. Ibrahim and a few of his friends pondered many questions as we shared the stories of the early church in the book of Acts. How does faith survive and flourish among persecuted believers? How can good truly overcome such evil? How can hope be maintained when darkness is all around us? How can peace make sense when persecution is severe?

We knew Christ's words in John 14:27: "Peace I leave with you; my peace I give you. I do not give to you as the world gives. Do not let your hearts be troubled and do not be afraid." Yet how can someone not let their hearts be troubled and have no fear when in a torture room?

While I could not always answer those questions, I shared how I found comfort and hope from Jesus' teaching in Matthew 5:11-12. He said, "Blessed are you when people insult you, persecute you and falsely say all kinds of evil against you because of me. Rejoice and be glad, because great is your reward in heaven, for in the same way they persecuted the prophets who were before you."

> I can testify that serving God is a matter of obedience through suffering.

That reward is the hope for suffering believers. I can testify that serving God is a matter of obedience through suffering.

We arrived in Sana'a in the afternoon. Ibrahim and Rahman had appointments with one of Ibrahim's business friends who wanted to meet privately, so I decided to visit with a few friends I had met previously, and then with a couple of underground secret believers that night. They were able to update me on the suffering of the believers there, as well as the need for prayers for their safety. Leaving Islam is forbidden in Yemen and other countries in the region. Muslims who decide to follow Jesus can face the death penalty. Even to this day, there is no tolerance for any open church activities or private worship. They told me that many followers of Christ were being abducted, and I was saddened to learn that some had even been killed when it was discovered that they were followers of Jesus. While I knew those believers were in heaven where Jesus said rewards awaited them, I was still troubled and angry about the persecution.

Trouble always creates questions. How do we maintain hope when darkness is all around us? Does the peace Jesus spoke of in John 14:27 make sense to believers who are being persecuted?

I've often been asked why God allows such evil to take place, and I honestly do not know the answer. The Bible does tell us that evil does not come from God, nor can we blame God for all the evils in the world. Evil comes from Satan, and it entered this world when Satan deceived Adam and Eve and caused them to turn against God (Genesis 3). Yet God can, and does, give us victory over evil. That doesn't mean bad things will never happen to us— but when they do, we can know the Lord is with us and will give us the strength to stand against them. Isn't it better to face life's problems with God than without Him?

The next day, the three of us met with the "men of peace" in Yemen who Ibrahim had connected me with before. They were mostly businessmen and Muslims. I noticed how Ibrahim wisely and carefully declared his new faith in God without saying he was a Christian to his Muslim friends. He always mentioned he was following the teachings of all the prophets, pointing out how the prophet Jesus had done miracles in his life. I also shared my stories of what God had done for me, then said that I had returned to meet with the religious leaders who had questioned and condemned me to prison in the past. I answered any questions the "men of peace" had, and I emphasized that I wanted to appreciate them and continue to be their friends.

When I had been released from prison previously in Yemen, the religious leader's verdict was that I could stay and serve, but never share my stories. Otherwise, I'd be deported. While I had humbly chosen to stay despite the humiliation it brought me, that decision had somehow lessened their hostility toward me. Though Ibrahim did not have any relationship with these religious leaders, his friends offered to go meet with them first to see if they were willing to meet with us. The religious leaders agreed, and we were invited for a tea ceremony the next afternoon at one of the leaders' homes.

We arrived, and to my surprise the meeting turned out to be a big, friendly Yemeni cuisine party with dishes of fahsa (stew) and foul, falafel cakes, and lamb and goat kebab with freshly baked flat-bread. We all sat in a circle eating communally, sharing bowls and using our right hands as is customary in that culture. They also offered me the addictive narcotic leaf they constantly chewed, but I politely declined. I was concerned how they would react to that, but they weren't offended. Instead, they just said I was missing the good stuff.

I pressed through my fear and uncertainty, sharing how it did not make sense to me how telling my story of God's deliverance the last time I was in Yemen was a crime that led to me being impris-oned. I expressed how disappointed and hurt I was by that, but I also declared my gratitude for my release and for being allowed to stay and serve because of the love I had for their people.

I then repeated how much I appreciated them, that their deci-sion to free me was an act of love, and that I forgave them for where I felt I had been wronged by them.

Everyone became silent.

One of the religious leaders asked, "How were you wronged?"

"For telling my story," I answered, hoping he didn't hear the panic I instantly felt inside.

Memories of my past suffering in prisons—deprivation of food and water, the beatings and electrocutions, being hung upside down, and even sexual torture—caused anger to rise within me. I also feared they might condemn me to prison again, right then and there.

My heartbeat raced. It was challenging to be in a room having a meal with people I knew had hurt me, knowing these issues had not yet been discussed. *Why am I here?* I questioned myself. *What am I doing?*

Then one of the other religious leaders spoke. "I remember when you worked here at the clinic for our sick people. You were allowed to do your work, but then you started converting our people to your false religion and having private meetings to teach doctrine that is forbidden. You also disrespected our culture, and you cannot come here to insult us," he said. "These crimes must be punished, and we had to have law enforcement officials discipline you. That was your wrong, and it is still your wrong, even after we had mercy on you."

I was more terrified and began to tremble. As things became tense, Ibrahim and his friends entered into the dialogue, acting as a reconciliatory team. I was so paralyzed with fear, I don't remember the back-and-forth discussion they had with one another. There was much bitterness in the room, and I was preoccupied as I mentally relived the pain I had experienced in prison, thinking they were going to throw me back in there. At that moment, I even considered the option of committing suicide rather than returning to the torture of that prison.

Things gradually quieted down, and I sat in silence and dread. After a few minutes, a different religious leader asked, "What do you need from us?" I heard the remorse in his voice, and without hesitation I responded.

"Please forgive me for my wrong!"

He continued. "We now know your intention and concerns for our people. You are our brother, and we know you have helped many of our sick people and care for our communities." He looked at Ibrahim. "Your friends have made us aware of your agenda of living at peace with everyone, and we accept that."

Then he looked back at me and added, "But you cannot break the law."

I watched them continue to talk among themselves with calm, friendlier tones, and I saw the smile from Ibrahim. I sensed things were going a little better, and I allowed myself to hope once more. One of the leaders hosting the gathering then said, "We are glad you came with your friend. You are welcomed here, and you are one of us."

Instantly, I was at peace and knew the trouble had passed. I was content to see it as some sort of a resolution. More tea was brought, and I was given the honor of filling my cup first.

The host repeated the question. "What do you need from us?"

My plan was to also visit the prison, donate food and water to the inmates who I knew were being deprived of those needs, and if possible, meet with the ruthless prison wardens who had tortured me. I calmly and confidently replied, "As I said earlier, I came to forgive the wrongs done against me and to ask for your forgiveness for my offenses. I believe in the forgiveness and love as taught by Jesus Christ. My request is permission to visit the prison where I was before. Aside from that, I am so thankful for your welcome and hospitality today."

Before we departed, one of the religious leaders told me, "May Allah forgive us, and we are sorry for how you were hurt." He then said they would consult and get back to us regarding the request to visit the prison.

> God reminded me that He has His way of doing things despite my anxiety and fears.

After the meeting, I was relieved, and that night, I was at peace. Again, God reminded me that He has His way of doing things despite my anxiety and fears. I recalled Paul's words in 2 Thessalonians 3:16. He wrote, "Now may the Lord of peace himself give you peace at all times and in every way. The Lord be with all of you."

The request to visit the prison was declined, and I accepted the decision of the authorities. To this day, I have never met with those cruel prison wardens, but I am thankful to remain casual friends with some of those religious leaders. I consider them "men of peace" in their community and their country—though they never talk about the continued oppression and persecution of Christians in their nation. Still, secret followers exist and are increasing in Yemen, even though it remains very dangerous to identify as a believer in Jesus.

We left Yemen two days later, after which I went to Kenya for a week to visit my family before returning to Belfast. Ibrahim and Rahman traveled back to their home in Morocco.

Before our separate flights departed from the airport in Dubai, Ibrahim, Rahman and I reviewed our visit to Sana'a. In the debriefing, Rahman asked, "How will disciples go to all the nations with severe persecution?" Ibrahim added, "What about believers who died and were never baptized or given holy communion?"

"Jesus Himself was persecuted, and His disciples were persecuted," I replied, "yet many years later, He has a few billion followers. There are many being persecuted, but that is no excuse to retreat or fear fulfilling His Great Commission. Surely, Jesus will be with us always, to the very end of the age."

We read Romans 8:35-39, which says, "Who shall separate us from the love of Christ? Shall trouble or hardship or persecution or famine or nakedness or danger or sword? As it is written: 'For your sake we face death all day long; we are considered as sheep to be slaughtered.' No, in all these things we are more than conquerors through him who loved us. For I am convinced that neither death nor life, neither angels nor demons, neither the present nor the future, nor any powers, neither height nor depth, nor anything else in all creation, will be able to separate us from the love of God that is in Christ Jesus our Lord."

We also took hope from Christ's words in Matthew 5:10, "Blessed are those who are persecuted because of righteousness, for theirs is the kingdom of heaven," as well as from Hebrews 10:39. It says, "But we do not belong to those who shrink back and are destroyed, but to those who have faith and are saved."

I had faith—but what happened next was going to surprise even me.

Chapter 10

HOPE SUSTAINED

We prayed, parted ways, and after going to Kenya, I returned to Belfast to raise funds for the trips still to come. It was a challenge because I was unable to get friends and churches to financially commit to my return to the places I had been imprisoned and abused. Therefore, I decided to look for short-term side jobs to generate the needed funds.

I contacted Tearfund and Samaritan's Purse to see if they could use me for a few months. While I waited to hear back from them, a friend who was on the missions committee of one of the churches that supported me approached me about a Sudanese ministry they were doing in Cairo, Egypt. Knowing my past experience serving in Sudan, they recruited me to be a part of a team going on a 10-day trip to a refugee camp in Cairo. The team was focused on discipleship and Bible distribution, and they also ran a medical clinic.

I agreed to go, and we arrived via British Airways in the evening. Early the next morning, we were in the camp and stayed each day into the afternoon to work around a 5:00 p.m. to 7:00 a.m. daily curfew for the refugees. On the third day, however, we remained in the camp two hours past curfew. As a result, our van was stopped just after 7:00 p.m. about a mile outside of the camp by the Cairo police.

I was the only dark-skinned member of the team. The police separated me from the others.

"Where are you from, and where are you going?" one of the officers asked.

"We were serving my brothers and sisters from Sudan," I stated calmly, "and we are going to where we lodge." When they inquired about my job, I responded that I was a missionary worker.

The police suspected that I was a Sudanese refugee trying to escape from the camp in disobedience to the curfew order. Even though I had a passport proving that I was not Sundanese, I was arrested anyway.

Upon arrival at the police station, I was interrogated and held in a cell overnight. The next morning, I was transferred to a detention center for two days. I was accused of lying to the arresting officers, of being Sudanese because I had referred to the refugees as "my brothers and sisters," of breaking the curfew order, and of being in the country as a missionary worker without a legal worker's permit.

Over those two days, I was beaten by the interrogators, and I was at a loss as to why I was being treated the way I was. My travel documents were not from Sudan. I also wondered, assuming the rest of the team were let go, if they were also considered to be mission workers. I was eventually given two options: remain in jail for a few months or receive lashes and be deported immediately.

I chose the lashes and deportation. I did not ask for, nor was I offered, a chance to meet with anyone on the mission team. At that point, I just wanted to leave.

I was driven to the airport and given my passport, but they did not give me my British Airways return ticket. My personal travel bag containing that ticket remained at the hotel. I was confused, angry, and in a lot of pain. Then, when I was placed on a flight with Egyptair, I believed that I was being deported back to London—but as the flight took off, I heard that it was headed instead to Lusaka, Zambia.

This made me more upset and befuddled. It also hurt to sit on my seat because of the lashes I'd received. There were no passengers on either side of me. I thought it was because I was stinky, wounded, and bleeding since I had not been given a chance to clean up after my incarceration.

A few minutes after takeoff, a woman completely covered with a hijab came up to me. Only her eyes were visible through the veil of her garment.

"Would you be okay with my husband sitting next to you so that one of our kids can stretch out to sleep?"

I didn't want to talk to her, or anyone else for that matter.

"Why would you want your husband to sit here?" I said angrily.

She left without replying—but five minutes later, a gentleman who introduced himself as Jamal Ahmed came and sat down next to me. He was the husband of the woman who had approached me earlier. Clearly, she took my terse response as a "yes."

We sat in silence for a while. Then he asked me, "Are you from Zambia?"

"No," I said. I asked him, "Are you from Egypt?"

"No. I am from Dubai for business, I am based in Zambia, but I am originally from Iran." Jamal then revealed that he owned businesses in five different countries.

I was sure he was going to get up and move because I smelled so bad. But then he asked what I was doing in Cairo. Knowing that he was a Muslim, I told him I was doing Kingdom business. He noticed that I was in pain and asked about it, so I told him about my suffering in Egypt.

As Jamal expressed genuine sympathy for me, I ended up sharing stories of my previous imprisonments in other Muslim countries. He was trying to figure out what I meant by "Kingdom" business, and I was being nice to him—but I was also hoping to irritate him enough that he'd leave. I just wanted to be by myself.

Jamal didn't get up to go sit with his family until about 40 minutes before the end of the flight. When he returned briefly once more, he handed me an envelope, then went back to his seat without another word.

I watched him depart, then looked at the envelope. I was more than skeptical. Maybe it was my ticket to London, or perhaps it was a document designed to get me into more trouble.

At that moment, I didn't trust anyone. But I still opened it.

To my surprise, it contained a check.

It was made out in British pound sterling.

It was for the exact, full amount of the budget I needed to return to the remaining countries I wanted to visit—the very money I had not been able to raise.

I was amazed and in awe. I had not said anything to Jamal about my intention to travel to those countries, much less shared anything about the funds I needed.

In my confusion, joy, and everything in between, I thought, *Is this real?* I wondered if the check was legitimate. *How could a complete stranger from another religion, whose fellow Muslims had imprisoned and tortured me, provide the money?*

> I was amazed and in awe.

Because Jamal had returned to his seat, I didn't say "thank you" or ask him what it was for—but I knew something unusual was happening. I had not eaten on the flight because I had lost my appetite, and I was weak, but the check somehow renewed my energy.

The plane landed at chaotic Kenneth Kaunda International Airport, and I disembarked with nothing else but my passport and the envelope. I had no idea where to go next. When I asked an

Egyptair attendant for help, he suggested I talk to an agent at the airline counter. As I headed that way, Jamal and his family walked by, and he handed me his business card.

"Please call me if you need anything," he said. He sounded concerned as they left.

The agent was not able to assist me, so I went to the British Airways counter, hoping they could get me on my way back to England. However, I did not have any proof of the previous return ticket, so they could not reroute me. I was stranded.

I stayed that way for the next 12 hours. As I waited at the airport all night, unable to sleep and often getting up and moving around, the uncertainty made me frantic, angry, and confused. I wondered what was going on at that moment with the rest of the team in Cairo. Did they even know where I was? I had no idea.

By mid-morning, I got out the business card and called Jamal using a phone at the British Airways counter. I quickly updated him on my situation, and he graciously returned to the airport, helped me through immigration, and took me to his house in Lusaka. Located about 10 miles from the airport, Jamal's home was opulent and huge, though I didn't see much of the inside. Out of respect and fear, I mostly stayed in the guest room and their living room. That's where we had our meals and spent time together.

That evening, Jamal purchased a one-way ticket for me to London on British Airways, but I had to wait three more days because British Airways only flew into Lusaka three days a week.

I could not sleep that night, or any of the next three nights, because of my anxiety. Anytime that I was alone, I prayed and wept. I missed my Bible, too. Jamal and his family were very hospitable to me, a hurting, stinky stranger they met on the plane. I marveled. *How can this be? An Iranian and a Muslim, caring for and being generous to me like I was a member of his family? This has to be God!*

I remembered that Jamal had mentioned that he disagreed with Christian beliefs, so I was afraid to engage his family in a conversation about anything religious. I wanted to just lay low until I departed, hoping the check from Jamal would clear when I returned to England. He invited me to pray with them a few times, and I did, but I was not able to kneel because my knees were hurting so much from the beating that I had endured in Cairo.

As we visited, Jamal not only told me about his upbringing in Iran, but he also introduced me to some of his close friends who were followers of Jesus in Iran. I talked with them over the phone at his house, and he was there with me for those conversations. Jamal also discussed how Christians in Iran are not free to worship and are punished if they are discovered. I thought it was odd that he was sharing that with me, yet when I asked him who was persecuting the Christian believers in Iran, he answered, "Narrow-minded government leaders."

I knew then that Jamal was not an extremist. From then on, I told him more about my ministry work, including details of the persecution I'd suffered in different countries. Jamal was moved, and he expressed his appreciation to me for sharing my stories with him.

Still unsure if I could really cash the check Jamal had gifted to me, I gracefully asked him to give me the funds in cash and write a letter from him as the originator of the funds just in case I got into trouble later in Belfast for trying to deposit such a large sum of money. Jamal agreed, and he gave me the money and the letter the night before my departure.

Incredibly, God had worked out His plans for me when I traveled to Egypt, was deported to Lusaka, and met Jamal Ahmed and his family in the process. God used him and the entire situation to provide all the travel funds I needed for the future without me having to get a side job or ask for any more donations.

Before Jamal took me to the airport, I asked if I could pray a blessing over him and his family. We prayed together, and it was such an emotional experience. Everyone was in tears, and I knew that God was doing something unique for all of us.

Then, as he dropped me off at the departure terminal, Jamal handed me another envelope.

"By the way," he said, "this one is for you to use to go visit my friends in Iran. They are like a family to me, and you will be a great encouragement to them." When I opened the envelope after passing through security, I saw that it was additional funds. I didn't know how much it would cost to visit Iran, but I was convinced it was God's provision and presented a new opportunity to minister.

Safely on the plane to London and then Belfast, I could not stop thinking of Philippians 4:19, which says, "And my God will meet all your needs according to the riches of his glory in Christ Jesus." A scenario that seemed out of control was completely in God's control. The devil had evil in mind for me in Cairo, yet God used it for good.

In the book of Genesis, Joseph went through one challenging time after another, but the Lord used it all to be a blessing for many, as well as to help Joseph heal and reconcile with his brothers. I had mixed emotions as I recalled the pain of my suffering and the happiness of God's providing care. I had just experienced the joy of serving the Sudanese, harm and hurt at the hand of the authorities in Cairo, and the fear and confusion of the flight from Egypt to Zambia. I was approached on that flight by a random woman in a hijab who sent her husband to me, and that had led to a miraculous provision.

All I could do was praise and trust God as I meditated on Philippians 4:6. "Do not be anxious about anything, but in every situation, by prayer and petition, with thanksgiving, present your requests to God."

In Belfast, I took some time to recover, rest, and reflect on everything God had done. I also learned that the mission team I had accompanied to Egypt had returned the day before I arrived back in England. They were safe, but they, too, were confused and hurting. I found out that they had been threatened while they were trying to find out where I was. The authorities did not tell them, but they returned with my luggage. I was glad when they visited and encouraged me. They had truly become ministry partners to reach the "least of these" with the love and hope of Jesus (Matthew 25:40).

During my recovery, I also started having regular phone conversations with Jamal's friends in Iran, and I began making plans to visit them using the funds Jamal had provided. I decided my first stop before going to Iran would be Afghanistan. I chose to delay my planned trips to Pakistan and Saudi Arabia until after I went to Iran because I did not yet have anyone to accompany me to those countries. I needed someone who could provide support and serve as a fluent language interpreter. I reached out to Ibrahim to see if he would be led to join me as I made arrangements with the "men of peace" in those places.

Three weeks after my return from Zambia, I left and arrived in Kabul, Afghanistan where I was hosted by Abdula Zahid and Rashad, the "men of peace" who had previously helped me be released from prison there. I stayed with them for three days, during which time they arranged for me to again meet with the prison officials whom I had sought forgiveness from before and now considered friends. We shared a meal and fellowship, and it was very friendly. I am thrilled to say that many of the people introduced to me by the prison officials, and many who I have met through the small groups they helped to organize for me, have come to accept Jesus Christ as their Savior. Most are secret believers today.

While in Afghanistan, I also met with the Ghazni police officers who had arrested me, and I visited the prison where I had been incarcerated. The "men of peace" arranged and facilitated the meeting with my jailers. Though confident and at peace, I wasn't sure how it was going to turn out. After meeting with them, the "men of peace" offered a long Islamic prayer, and the conversation in the room was in their language, Pashto, so I did not know what was being said.

Eventually, two of the officers stood up, shook my hand, and hugged me. Each of them said, "May Allah forgive us."

I responded, "I forgive all that was done, and may God's grace be upon us." I saw genuineness in their faces and heard it in the tone of their voices.

It was a pleasant and godly atmosphere—and my heart was filled with joy knowing what God had just done. I thought of Psalm 92:4. "For you make me glad by your deeds, Lord; I sing for joy at what your hands have done." I was simply content to **"I forgive all that was done, and may God's grace be upon us."** enjoy that moment with my captors, even if we didn't go through a deeper reconciliatory process. I understood they had done much, according to their faith, to make things right.

Two days later, I returned to Belfast for rest, reflection, and preparation to go to Iran, Pakistan, and Saudi Arabia. During this time, I corresponded further with Jamal's friends in Iran. After getting to know each other, we knew it was God's divine connection. I learned more about their oppression as secret followers of Christ, and they shared how they were interested in learning about discipleship and wanted to know if followers of Jesus in other parts of the world were as oppressed as they were in Iran. When I arrived in the Iranian capital of Tehran for a weeklong visit, I was received by Jamal's friends. It was as if we had known each other for years and I was a part of their family.

I was! We were in God's family, and I felt the Holy Spirit in them and sensed the richness of their deep faith in Christ.

We had a wonderful time of fellowship, and in the process, I witnessed the pressure of being a follower of Jesus in Iran. Christians there were forbidden from sharing their faith with non-Christians. Secret house churches were monitored and frequently raided, and many followers of Jesus there have been imprisoned, tortured, or threatened with death. Both the Armenian and Assyrian churches were allowed to practice their faith openly as long as they were not conducted in Farsi (the most common language in Iran), and they were often observed by the police. Distributing Christian literature in Farsi was strictly forbidden, and it was illegal for believers to share the gospel in any way with Muslims.

Converts from Islam in Iran faced persecution from the government. If they attended secret house churches, they were prosecuted and sentenced to lengthy jail terms. Others awaited trial. Meanwhile, their families faced public humiliation. Arrested believers who managed to raise enough bail money for a conditional release forfeited that money if they then proceeded to flee the country. Most believers from Muslim backgrounds kept their faith a secret.

On my fourth day visiting Jamal's friends, we discussed Christ's Great Commission from Matthew 28:18-20. That encouraged them, and they vowed to continue reaching out and making disciples, even with the constant threat of capital punishment. They also realized that they did not need to be ordained, government-licensed priests to baptize other believers. Jesus gave that authority to all His disciples.

They then asked me to baptize them, and I passionately did so at the family pool that evening.

It was such an honor. There was such great joy, I did not even think or care about the possible danger of our actions.

Early the next morning, there was a raid at the house where I was being hosted, and I was arrested along with the host family. I did not understand Farsi, so I was not sure what was being said until I was at the police station where I was interrogated in English. I was accused of "crimes against national security." I didn't know what that meant, but I learned it came with a long prison sentence.

All-too-familiar doubts and fears arose within me as I remembered my previous imprisonments and abuse. Knowing there was no way around my situation, I settled in my mind that I was going to prison. But when I asked if I could explain what happened at the family pool, they gave me a chance to speak.

That's when I fabricated a story. It was clever, perhaps, but not true.

"I am not sure if you have heard," I said, "but black people tend to sink. We never float, and we struggle to swim. I was curious if that was the case in a pool in Iran. Since I didn't sink, I decided to test to see if my friends would stay down if I pulled them deep into the water. One after another, they came back up, and we enjoyed playing that way."

I continued, "My intention was not to do any religious act or commit any crime during my visit here, sir. Please forgive me for testing this black sinking voodoo during my visit."

The two interrogating officers looked at each other.

"That makes sense," one of them replied, then looked back at me and asked, "We *have* heard that black people don't swim. Why is that?"

At that point, I knew my made-up story was working in my favor.

"Sir, that is something I would like to go ask my dad when I return home this week, and I promise to return and tell you what he says."

Incredibly, I was released and ordered never to play that game in Iran ever again. I escaped prison time, even though I was still beaten a bit during the interrogation. Most of the others who had been baptized were arrested for misconduct and released, but they later escaped to Turkey due to increased persecution. The fate of the others baptized that night remains unknown. It was feared they were killed.

I have since returned to Iran and visited the growing secret churches there, but I never went back to the police station to tell them why black people don't swim. When I later visited my father, I told him this story.

"Son," he said, "you are a weird, odd, and funny preacher. I cannot believe those Arabs or Persians let you get away with it. You come up with stories most of the people never think of in situations like that. I am glad you are alive."

To be called a weird and odd preacher was not a compliment when I was growing up, but my dad can say whatever he thinks now that I'm an adult—and, for the record, I can swim. I always have.

If I could name two places I never wanted to visit again, they were Saudi Arabia and Pakistan. While I had no doubt God had told me to go back to them, I struggled with it so much that when it seemed funds were not going to come in to finance the trips, I thought maybe the Lord had changed His mind. Then I met Jamal Ahmed, God provided through him, and there was no way I couldn't go. It was just a matter of scheduling and strategizing the meetings.

It was hard to forget the horrific abuses and suffering I'd experienced in those two countries, but I also could not stop embracing how God had so miraculously released me from each of those prisons. So, I knew the Lord was going to have His way through me, make Himself known, and be glorified.

I asked Ibrahim to go with me, but he could not make the trip to either country, so I reached out to my friend, Ruben. He was from Holland, and I had met him years earlier at a mission conference in Amsterdam. He was working with Open Door Mission in the Middle East, and he had previously wanted me to travel with him there. We also had some common friends in that region. Gratefully, Ruben was willing to join me in Pakistan, but not in Saudi Arabia.

I scheduled my trip, first to Riyadh, Saudi Arabia, and then to Pakistan where Ruben would join me before I returned to Belfast. I first reached out to the friends who had invited me to Saudi Arabia, and I also connected with Sheikh Nasser, the Imam who had taken such good care of me at his home after I had been released from Al-Ha'ir prison. Knowing he was a "man of peace" and a friend I could trust, I felt visiting him and telling him about my desire to see my captors was a good idea. I also hoped he might be able to facilitate my return to that prison, and perhaps even join me so I wouldn't be alone when I saw the jailers.

It made me happy to hear he was excited about my visit. A respected Muslim preacher, Sheikh Nasser had strong connections with the Saudi king and was a busy man. I felt honored that he was able to create time for my stay, and I looked forward to thanking him further for the love, hospitality, and care he had shown me at one of the lowest points of my life.

We met at the hotel the evening of my arrival. He came, along with a few others, after evening prayers. I took time to share with him my appreciation for his friendship and to tell him about my desire to visit the prison and, if possible, to meet the wardens who were in charge during my incarceration at Al-Ha'ir. I told him all about the forgiveness and healing I had experienced. "I would like to extend the same forgiveness and healing to the wardens and anyone else who was involved in placing me in prison," I said.

He was quick to respond. "What are your intentions about what happened in the past? Why do you want to readdress what was resolved in your favor? You were forgiven and even let go. It's unwise to revisit this, and it may not work in your favor this time."

I heard Sheikh Nasser clearly and immediately knew in my heart that I should not pursue anything else beyond utilizing my time with him to understand more about forgiveness from his perspective as an Islamic scholar.

As we continued to meet and have tea together, I decided to use the writings of the Quran to help further explain why I wanted to meet with those who had hurt me. "Your Scripture says to call the one who is disputing with you and treat him nicely." I then quoted Quran 24:22 (Saheeh International). "'Would you not like that Allah should forgive you? And Allah is Forgiving and Merciful.' Perhaps this might be a reason, after the mercy of Allah Almighty, for forgiveness?"

"That's my intent," I said. "I want to have God's mercy and forgiveness with everyone."

One of the other men who came with the Imam, Ahmad, spoke up. "You are trying to be the one who takes the initiative of reconciliation. The Prophet said, 'It is unlawful for a Muslim to forsake his fellow Muslim for more than three consecutive days. When they meet, each of them turns his face away from the other. The better one is the one who starts the greeting.' But there is an issue with the Prophet's teaching concerning you."

I asked the Sheikh Nasser to explain.

"The Muslim is the brother of another Muslim; he neither oppresses him nor humiliates, lies, or holds him in contempt. It is enough evil for a person to hold his brother Muslim in contempt. The role of a Muslim for another Muslim is sacred; his blood, his property, and his honor," the Imam replied. "But you are not a Muslim, Tabib Okongo.

He continued. "There are people who went to sit with their opponents for only twenty or thirty minutes, but they ended up sitting for long hours because of the great happiness, comfort, familiarity, and love they felt when meeting those who wronged them. But I do not think this will happen in your case."

With that, I did not need any more details, and I did not want to meet my captors at Al-Ha'ir. To this day, I have not met any of them, but I remain so thankful for the clarity I gained from Sheikh Nasser and his friends who gracefully made me aware that I needed to move on. The peace of God filled me, and I am still blessed with the friendship of the Imam and by his wisdom, even though we have different beliefs and faiths.

As of 2021, Saudi Arabia allows Christians to enter the country as foreign workers for work or tourism. Most followers of Christ there are migrants, and there are a few Muslim-born believers as well as some who are secret converts like Majid, Saleh, and Ahmed. All are doing outreach there, and it is very dangerous. Conversion from Islam is punishable by death if discovered, and public practice of any form of religion other than Islam is illegal. However, Saudi authorities do accept private practice of religions other than Islam, and religious texts such as the Bible are allowed into the country as long as they are for personal use only. Followers of Christ meet in house churches, but they are frequently raided.

After my stay in Saudi Arabia was completed, I arrived next in Islamabad, Pakistan before taking another short flight from there to Quetta. Ruben met me two days later after I had taken some time to rest. During that break, I also communicated with the "men of peace" there that Ibrahim and I had befriended in the past. He hoped they could serve as mediators for me if I was able to meet with my captors in Pakistan, but they were mostly hesitant because of the differences in religious belief and practice when it came to the subject of reconciliation.

It was hard to forget the atrocities I'd experienced in Pakistan, and I had not been able to determine the whereabouts of my translators, Yousuf and Nazir, who had been arrested with me. Yet in my deepest fear and worry, I encouraged myself with Hebrews 10:23. "Let us hold fast the confession of our hope without wavering, for He who promised is faithful." (NKJV)

I was convinced God was going to keep His promise to not forsake me.

I was so glad to have Ruben with me to achieve the two-by-two travel modeled by Christ's disciples. Ruben had a connection  with a Catholic priest involved with prison ministry in Quetta, and we arranged to

I was convinced God was going to keep His promise.

meet with him. The priest distributed food and other needed items to prisoners weekly, and he was respected for being a bridge builder between religions. He also knew the story of my previous imprisonment there. I instantly felt the priest could help me in my goal to meet with my captors, and I also wanted to hear his advice about the matter.

Prior to our meeting with the priest, Ruben and I saw a few friends I had met earlier during my trips there with Tearfund and my visit with Ibrahim. It was great to catch up with them, and I also talked on the phone with other friends I had met previously in Karachi to hear how their ministry was progressing. Everyone expressed their deep concern about me going to the prisons and meeting my captors. To their knowledge, no one had ever tried to do that before. But they also understood that God was leading me.

Ruben and I then got together with two of the "men of peace" Ibrahim had spoken to regarding my visit, and we had a lengthy dialogue. They told me that they saw my desire to visit the prisons and my captors as being a government affair and law related instead of a being a person-to-person affair.

Once again, I chose to use the Quran during our discussion. "The Quran tells us, 'If you pardon, Allah Almighty will increase your honor; if you reconcile people, Allah Almighty will increase your honor. If you were expelled and you returned, then know that this is one of the wishes of your prophet because it is proof of the purity of the heart.' I believe in God to forgive and reconcile," I said. "Quran 49:10 states, "All believers are but brothers, therefore seek reconciliation between your two brothers, and fear Allah, so that you may be blessed with mercy." (Mufti Taqi Usmani) I am seeking God's mercy. Quran 24:22 says, "'Would you not like that Allah should forgive you? And Allah is Forgiving and Merciful.'" (Saheeh International)

I hoped the "men of peace" would understand my desire to show forgiveness to those who hurt me—but they were quick to dismiss my argument because I was not an Islam scholar qualified to interpret the Quran.

"According to our Islam teaching, the one who seeks reconciliation should keep the etiquettes of settlement in mind so that Allah Almighty supports him and so that he receives the fruits of his endeavor," they explained. "You appear to have intentional sincerity for the sake of Allah Almighty, and you appear to seek the countenance of Allah Almighty. Yet you are not a Muslim."

They went on to say that reconciliation is based upon Sharia knowledge, the Islamic religious law that governs not only religious rituals but also aspects of day-to-day life in Islam. "Islam permits us to study the issue from all sides and listen to each of the parties, but in your case, it was the breaking of the law that got you into prison. Yet you want to reconcile with the people there? Even the prison officers were doing what the law asked them to do," they said.

"You are non-Muslim, and per Islam, you are considered an unbeliever in an outward sense because you do not practice Islam. You follow different religious laws and perform different rites regarding prayers, healing, forgiveness, and many other things. Per our faith, we only judge your outward deeds and not your heart." They concluded, "It is not permissible by Islam to declare you to be an absolute dweller of the Hellfire for your wrong, since only Allah knows your true situation. Rather, we should leave this to Allah alone."

There was no doubt: the "men of peace" were not willing to agree with me, but they did offer some excellent advice. They encouraged me to go to the prison with food items as gifts, but not try to have dialogue with the wardens or anyone else there who instigated my earlier arrest and abuse.

Then, surprisingly, one of the "men of peace" asked to pray as we were finishing our meeting.

"O Allah, purify our hearts from grudge, envy, and injustice. O Allah, amend our relations with our relatives and all others. O Allah, amend our relations with our loved ones. O Allah, make life an increase for us in every good, and make death a relief for us from every evil with your mercy, O Most Merciful of the Merciful."

While I appreciated the prayer, the way it ended scared me. I was not prepared to hear anything about death being a relief. The idea instantly made me anxious as I pondered what was really meant by those words.

Ruben said he did not understand that prayer, either, but at least he was not afraid.

I took courage from that.

The next day, Ruben and I met with the Catholic priest and decided to join him for his prison ministry visit that week. The priest had teamed up with a few other area churches to do the outreach. Back when I was first imprisoned there, I did not recall seeing the priest or anyone from his team, but I love it when believers serve in unity (Psalm 133:1). Once we arrived at the prison, Ruben and I joined the priest and another member of his team, a Pakistani interpreter, serving meals and praying with prisoners.

We then went to the warden's office.

I couldn't tell if the prison officers who were there were the ones who had tortured me. Everyone looked alike to me. Still, after a few moments of conversation, I spoke up.

"I came to express my forgiveness for what had happened to me and the harm that was done to me. Forgiveness is what has healed me from the wounds I had."

Ruben and the priest listened quietly as my words were repeated through the interpreter.

The jail superintendent slapped the table. The loud smack reverberated through the room.

"Ma Allaena!" he yelled in Arabic.

In English, the term is translated, "What the f**k!"

That split second, I fell to the ground on my knees and pled for mercy.

Every emotion from the pain I'd experienced when I was last imprisoned there flooded back.

I was in deep trouble.

The jail superintendent delivered a harsh order to two of the guards. They came over, pulled me up, and took me to the room next to his office. Alone, confused, and frightened, I silently cursed myself, *Why did I come to meet with him? Why am I seeking forgiveness from someone I cannot even recognize? Why did I not listen to the advice from the "men of peace?" I am so stupid and unwise!* I was so angry with myself. *Even my friends had warned me. Why didn't I listen to God through their concerns?*

I had no clue what Ruben, the priest, and his team member were experiencing next door. But only one thought raced through my mind.

I'm going back to prison—and this time I'll be beheaded or burned!

I had never, ever been so afraid.

As I struggled to compose myself, I began to pray for God to rescue me. I remembered the words of Hebrews 11:5. "By faith Enoch was taken from this life, so that he did not experience death: 'He could not be found, because God had taken him away.' For before he was taken, he was commended as one who pleased God."

I begged the Lord to take me away as He had Enoch. I wanted Him to blow the roof off of the building and pull me out so that I didn't have to face certain death.

The words of the "man of peace" haunted me.

"Make death a relief for us from every evil with your mercy."

Could it be that his prayer is about to come to pass?

I remained in that room by myself, pleading and desperate, for 30 minutes.

God did not whisk me away as He had Enoch.

Finally, I heard the door open and saw the guards. They grabbed me and took me to yet a different room. Inside were Ruben, the priest, and two other prison officers.

With them was the jail superintendent who had cussed at us.

"We are going to have a meeting at my home," he declared.

I was trembling and my voice was just as shaky. "Yes, sir!"

I had no idea what was going to happen.

But at least his house is not the prison, I thought.

I rode with Ruben and the priest, with the jail superintendent's car in front of us and another prison vehicle behind. As we went from one street to another, Ruben and the priest kept encouraging me and ministering to me. I was completely traumatized and could not stop shaking.

Everything changed once we got to the jail superintendent's house.

We were welcomed inside, and the jail superintendent who had earlier swore and slapped the table now addressed us gently and with grace. We gathered in his living room, and the dialogue that followed was awkward—we talked about the different cultures I'd encountered on my travels, as well as about our families—and I was reluctant to share too much about anything.

Then, as food was served, I was shocked when one of the "men of peace" from the previous meeting joined us.

He was not the one who had prayed about death.

Discussion continued, and I quietly offered my own prayer from Deuteronomy 31:6. "Be strong and courageous. Do not be afraid or terrified because of them, for the Lord your God goes with you; he will never leave you nor forsake you." I forced myself to eat, knowing that being offered food was an act of reconciliation. A part of me wondered if it was poisoned, but I ate anyway. It was good food: biryani, khadi kabab (goat) with rice, dried fruits served alongside naan bread, and chai tea.

When the meal was completed, the jail superintendent looked at me and smiled.

"I apologize for how I reacted earlier. Please forgive me of any wrong I caused you."

I was amazed, but I didn't seek any further explanation. "It's okay," I replied, "and please forgive me for anything I did wrong, and for any bitterness, anger, or hate that was not pleasing to God."

He and the other prison officer responded simultaneously, "May Allah have mercy."

Instantly, I was relieved.

I also wanted to leave.

But that was not to be. The priest then spoke of the power of forgiveness from a Christian perspective, saying that what he had just witnessed was God demonstrating love between His people. Ruben also encouraged everyone, saying that what he saw was an example of following Christ.

The "man of peace" then opened the Quran and read from Quran 2:62. "The [Muslim] believers, the Jews, the Christians, and the Sabians – all those who believe in God and the Last Day and do good – will have their rewards with their Lord. No fear for them, nor will they grieve." (Abdul Haleem) He continued with other passages: Quran 2:38, which says, "and whoever follows My Guidance, there shall be no fear on them, nor shall they grieve." (Muhsin Khan). No fear or grief is a description of life after death, the equivalent of God's salvation. It's the reward of those who follow God's guidance. "Whoever submits himself completely to the obedience of Allah and does good will find his reward with his Lord. No fear shall come upon them, nor shall they grieve." (Quran 2:112) (Tafheem-ul-Quran – Abul Ala Maududi)

He then told me, "Those who submit with faith have reward. May Allah reward you for your faith, Okwongo."

To this day, he cannot pronounce my name correctly.

The jail superintendent then made a confession. He admitted that he was the one, during my previous imprisonment, who had issued the order for me to be beheaded—but he could not explain why I was not killed. Watching him tell that story with tears in his eyes made me cry uncontrollably. Others in the room wept with us. We then hugged one another.

On the drive back to the hotel, I thought of 2 Chronicles 15:7. "But as for you, be strong and do not give up, for your work will be rewarded."

I realized it had been God's plan for me to return to Pakistan. He had divine plans prepared for Ruben and the Catholic priest.

He also divinely planned to have the "men of peace" share what they did so He could fulfill what only He could do.

Through it all, God glorified Himself.

I maintain my friendship with the jail superintendent. He is now retired, enjoying his family, and is a follower of Jesus. The jail superintendent has discipled many others and was involved in the priest's prison min-

Through it all, God glorified Himself.

istry. He was not able to introduce me to the specific guard who had tortured me, but I understand the confidentially of their work.

I am also thankful for the friendship of the "men of peace" and their families, and for Ruben's love for the Lord and his willingness to take the risk and time to accompany me. Because of him, I better understand Christ's words from John 13:35. "By this everyone will know that you are my disciples, if you love one another."

Today, the number of followers of Christ in Pakistan is growing.

I will not cease to sing Psalm 103:2-3. "Let all that I am praise the Lord; may I never forget the good things he does for me. He forgives all my sins and heals all my diseases." (NLT)

My journey as a follower of Christ and His calling upon my life have enabled me to meet others who abused me in Somalia, Libya, Sudan, Kenya, Jordan, Syria, Lebanon, Algeria, and Iraq. With each one, I have sought forgiveness and healing. Some offenders have never acknowledged any hurt they imposed on me but have justified their actions. Others have accepted my forgiveness, confessed their wrongdoing, and become my friends.

God has continued to allow us to serve with secret followers of Christ in those countries, and we see the Lord moving and drawing many to Himself. I have learned, and continue to learn, how to serve among different people with humility. I am honored to be used in any way that will give God the glory, even in my weakness.

I still remember the words God spoke to me that night so long ago: "I want to use you to the uttermost parts of the world to bring transformation to many people who are in need spiritually, socially, emotionally, physically, and economically, and to bring healing. You will go through challenges."

I still remember the vision He gave of me with crowds of people in different countries around the world.

I continue to follow His call and fulfill His vision.

I still want to go.

While I know many new challenges are ahead, I also know something else—beyond any shadow of a doubt.

God has not forsaken me, and He never will.

Epilogue

A LESSON IN FORGIVING–
EVEN WHEN IT FEELS IMPOSSIBLE

Forgiveness is a difficult topic. I say "difficult" because forgiving those who deeply hurt me has been the hardest challenge I have ever faced. But deciding to forgive them was unquestionably one of the most important choices I have ever made.

You can actually forgive someone who has hurt you, and that act of forgiveness will help you find freedom from unhealthy emotions that trap you in bitterness, anger, and hate.

It is important to note that forgiving your offender does *not* make what they did right and okay. By forgiving, you decide to let go of the resentment and indignation while creating and maintaining your boundaries. You may not feel like forgiving someone, but forgiveness is a choice.

It is also vital to understand what forgiveness is and what it is not. As we have done healing prayer ministry across the globe through Unite 4 Africa, I have listened to people's misconceptions about forgiveness. They mirror the misconceptions I've had about forgiveness, many of which were revealed in the story you just read in this book.

Forgiveness does not mean you are pardoning or excusing the other person's actions. Sometimes you don't need to tell the person they are forgiven. Forgiveness also doesn't mean there is nothing further to work out in the relationship or that everything is fine. Forgiveness doesn't mean you shouldn't still have feelings about the situation or that you forget the incident ever happened. You don't have to be friendly with or even include the forgiven person in your life, even though God led and enabled me to do that with some of my offenders, many of whom now serve with me in ministry. Still, forgiving someone doesn't necessarily mean you have to reconcile with them. God will show you the path to reconciliation as you allow Him to lead you.

Forgiveness is something you do for you, not just for the person who hurt you. After you are wronged and the initial painful wave of emotion has passed, you are left with a challenge. "Do I forgive the person?" This can be a gradual process—and it doesn't necessarily have to even include the person you are forgiving. God requires you to forgive, and by forgiving, you are letting go of your grievances and judgments, allowing yourself to heal. As you relinquish your right to harbor and hold onto the offense, you deny yourself (Matthew 16:24). The forgiveness is then experienced inside your heart, cleansing you of your sense of hatred and indignation so you can heal and move on with your life.

While this may sound so easy, forgiveness can sometimes feel impossible because the hurt went too deep or because the person was too abusive or expressed no regret. Therefore, do not attempt to forgive someone until after you have identified and fully felt, expressed, and released your anger and pain. In my story, people like Dickson and Dr. Pede helped me through that process, allowing me to understand and know how the grievous hurt was so disrupting my inner peace. Before that, it was difficult for me to concentrate on anything other than my turmoil and pain. When we hold on to our hurt, we are hobbled emotionally and cognitively, and our relationships suffer as a result. When life hits us that hard, there is nothing more effective than forgiveness for healing deep wounds. Forgiveness is strong medicine for the soul.

So, even when forgiveness feels impossible, I believe there are healthy steps you can take that worked for me in my journey of forgiveness and healing. I pray that you will think about how you can adopt them and put them to use in your own life.

Why forgiveness matters

Forgiveness is about goodness, extending grace and mercy to those who have hurt you, even if they don't deserve it. It is not a quick fix formula you can follow, but it is a process with many steps that often unfolds in a non-linear fashion as the Lord leads you.

Forgiveness matters because it can help you increase your self-esteem and sense of worth, and it provides inner strength and safety. Forgiveness can reverse the lies that you often tell yourself when someone has hurt you deeply—lies like, "I am *not good enough*," or "*I'm not worthy*," or "*Something is wrong with me*." Forgiveness can heal you and propel you forward with meaning and purpose. Forgiveness also allows you to hear God's voice over your hurt and pain, and it establishes a connection with Him that unforgiveness cuts off.

Many people are afraid to forgive. As a result, they embrace anger to protect themselves so they will not be vulnerable to pain ever again. Learning to trust God as your protector, and finding ways to believe He will reward you even if you suffer, is essential to release the other person who hurt you from their debt against you. As you forgive, you also become its beneficiary. Forgiveness decreased my depression, anxiety, unhealthy anger, and symptoms of PTSD. Forgiveness led to my emotional, spiritual, and psychological healing, and it will do the same for you.

As you extend forgiveness toward others, it means you've come to recognize that it is the best response to the situation. It can be tempting to play the blame game when you've been hurt, placing all of the responsibility on the offender. Often people tell me, *"I'm not going to reach out unless they do."* Yet that mentality does not help you because you are placing your ability to heal in someone else's control. By deciding to forgive, you put yourself in the position of power. Yes, you are hurt, but you allow yourself to progress whether or not they have acknowledged their sin. After all, forgiveness can't be forced, and God is sovereign in human relationships (Genesis 50:20). That is why you have to choose it for yourself when you are ready to accept what happened, acknowledge your feelings, and let go.

Acknowledge your inner pain

It's important to identify who has hurt you and how. I know many who were abused when they were young, but it is manifesting itself in their current life situation. Carefully look at the people in your life—your spouse, children, parents, siblings, peers, coworkers, and even yourself—and figure out how much each one has hurt you. Maybe they exercised power over you, rejected you, physically harmed you, or withheld their love from you. These hurts have contributed to your inner emotional pain and need to be recognized. Doing this will give you an idea of who needs forgiveness in your life and how to start addressing them.

Emotional pain can be caused by abuse, anxiety, depression, unhealthy anger, lack of trust, low self-esteem, an overall negative worldview, and a lack of confidence in your ability to change. All of these can be addressed by forgiveness, so it's important to identify the kind of pain you are suffering from and acknowledge it. The more hurt you have incurred, the more important it is to forgive, at least for the purpose of experiencing your own emotional healing. When I acknowledged my pain, I made every effort to visit as many captors as I could, even when I did not feel like doing so, remembering that reconciliation was a separate issue. One person can forgive, but it takes two people to reconcile. God showed me what I needed to do with my captors, and I believe He will show you what you need to do and lead you.

Seek help when forgiveness is hard

Remember, while you may be able to do this on your own, don't hesitate to get the help of others along the way. Forgiveness is always hard when you are dealing with deep injustices from others. I know some people who even refuse to use the word "forgiveness" because it makes them so upset and bitter. That's okay—we all have our own timelines for when we can be merciful. But if you want to forgive and are finding it challenging to do, seek help from others such as a trusted spiritual leader or a counselor with godly principles.

Struggling to forgive does not mean you are a failure at offering forgiveness. Forgiveness is a process that takes time, patience, and determination. Surround yourself with good and wise people who will support you and who have the patience to allow you time to heal in your own way. Practice humility, not in the sense of putting yourself down, but in realizing that all of us are capable of imperfection that can cause suffering.

When to say, "I forgive you."

If you are going to forgive someone who hurt you, the desire to let them know you have forgiven them is understandable. But before you do, keep in mind that when you say, "I forgive you," you are implying that they have indeed wronged you. If they don't understand this, you might offend them and set yourself up to be hurt again. They may say, "You forgive me? For what?"

Forgiveness should be offered to a person after they have understood or acknowledged their part in how you felt hurt, or have even apologized, confessed, or at least taken responsibility or offered to make amends with you. If you decide to have a conversation with the person, I encourage you to use 'I' language instead of 'you' language as you share your feelings and how you were hurt. For example, the statements, "You hurt me by your words," and "I was hurt by your words" each come across differently. You can do this even if the offender cannot or will not acknowledge their part in the offense.

Remember, too, that forgiveness is a personal and internal process, so there's no requirement to tell the person you've forgiven them, especially if you have cut off contact with them for your own well-being. Forgiveness is still required to God, whether or not a conversation with the offender ever takes place. Maybe the offender is unsafe, unreachable (which was my case with the LRA), or deceased. If you have freed yourself of the anger, pain, and hurt that was once weighing you down, you have already forgiven them. God leads people differently. He led me to some of my captors for His sake, which resulted in many becoming followers of Jesus. In those cases, forgiveness was not only for me, but for their lives to be transformed for eternity.

Find empathy

As I examined some of the details in the lives of the people who hurt me, I often saw the wounds they carried and started to develop empathy for them. You may be able to see their physical, emotional, spiritual, and psychological suffering, and begin to understand the common humanity that you share. You might well recognize the vulnerable person who was wounded and then wounded you in return. Despite what they may have done to hurt you, you realize that they did not deserve to suffer, either.

Recognizing that we all carry wounds in our hearts can help open the door to forgiveness. I find it helpful to try to see the story from someone else's viewpoint. I discovered that some of my captors and persecutors had sins of ignorance about what they were doing. Some were performing their duty as stipulated by the law or pressure from their religion. Some acted sinfully out of their deep brokenness and did evil things in their blindness. Understanding where someone is coming from helps you replace negative, unforgiving emotions such as hostility and bitterness with positive emotions like sympathy and compassion. You can see them as a tragedy that needs to be pitied.

I approached each abuser in my path to forgiveness with the belief that they may not have known what they did, just like Jesus did on the cross (Luke 23:34). Jesus had empathy and compassion toward His persecutors. This helped me to choose positive emotions, have fewer negative ones, and remember that I, too, have been forgiven. Doing this for yourself will bring freedom and make it easier to keep your emotions under control. It may even provide a fresh perspective to the situation that'll better help you come to terms with it.

In the end, those who have hurt you may suffer far more in this life, or in the one to come, because of their violations against you. This doesn't mean you excuse their behavior, but it does show how desperately they are in need of compassion. One great way to show compassion is to pray for the person who has hurt you (Matthew 5:44). Jesus knows it is impossible to pray for someone and continue to hate them. Then, while you're praying, ask for God to bring a blessing to their life. Ask for good things to come to them. Wish them well.

Discover the meaning in your suffering

When you suffer a great deal, it is important that you find meaning in what you have endured. Without this, you can lose a sense of purpose, which can lead to hopelessness and a despairing conclusion that there is no meaning to life at all. That doesn't mean that you should look for suffering in order to grow or try to find goodness in another's bad actions. Instead, try to discover how your suffering has changed you in a positive way to conform you more to the image of Christ.

It is possible to find a calling for your life in your suffering. As you begin to think about how you can use your suffering to cope, you become braver and more resilient. You may also realize that your suffering has altered your perspective regarding what is important in life, redefining how God can use you. What is meant for evil can be used for good by your God.

To find meaning in suffering is not to diminish your pain or resign yourself to just make the best of it because all things happen for a reason. Instead, it is to adopt a biblical mindset toward your suffering. As Romans 5:3-5 declares, "Not only so, but we also glory in our sufferings, because we know that suffering produces perseverance; perseverance, character; and character, hope. And hope does not put us to shame, because God's love has been poured out into our hearts through the Holy Spirit, who has been given to us." Use your suffering to become more loving and to pass that love on to others in the form of hope.

Develop a forgiving heart

When we overcome suffering, we gain a better understanding of what it means to be humble, courageous, and loving. This may enable you to create an atmosphere of forgiveness in your home, community, and workplace, to help others who are hurting be able to overcome their own suffering. This may result in protection from cycles of hatred and violence. Developing a forgiving heart can bring hope and joy to the hearts and lives of others.

Some believe that loving another person who hurt you is impossible. But I know many people who, once they forgive, find a way to open their hearts even more. If you get rid of bitterness and rage and put love in its place, then repeat this with many other people, you become freed to love others more widely and deeply. That is what happened to me when I returned to meet my captors. This kind of transformation will create a legacy of love that lives on long after we are gone.

Forgiving yourself

Most of us tend to be harder on ourselves than we are on others, struggling to love ourselves. If you are not feeling lovable because of actions you have taken, you may need to work on self-forgiveness and offer to yourself what you offer to others who have hurt you: a sense of inherent worth, despite your actions.

In self-forgiveness, you honor yourself as a person, even if you are imperfect. After you have been able to forgive yourself, you will also need to engage in seeking forgiveness from others whom you have hurt and right the wrongs as best as you can. This kind of humility invites safety rather than being a threat. It's important to be prepared for the possibility that the other person may not be ready to forgive you. If this is the case, you will need to practice patience and humility. But, a sincere apology, free of conditions and expectations, will go a long way toward helping you forgive yourself.

Practicing forgiveness is possible if you have worked on positively changing your inner person by trusting God and His Word on how to forgive. This can also enable you to make a commitment to do no harm, making a conscious effort not to talk disparagingly about those who have hurt you. I know this is hard. You don't have to say good things, but if you refrain from talking negatively, it will feed and inspire the more forgiving side of your mind and heart. Feeding negativity through rumor and gossip only causes more harm.

You can also recognize that every person is unique, special, and irreplaceable before your God despite their sins. I found a clear understanding of forgiveness from the Bible and became more inspired to take action. It's important to cultivate a mindset of valuing our common humanity, so that it becomes harder to discount someone who has hurt you as being unworthy. Sometimes pride and power can weaken your efforts to forgive by making you feel entitled, which may cause you to hang onto your resentment. When you find yourself in that place, choose forgiveness or mercy, and be sure to seek the help of others. If you need inspiration, the Bible will provide it (as it did for me).

In the end, forgiving others is a spiritual, supernatural exercise. I find it impossible to truly forgive others without God's help. God can help you forgive because not only has He forgiven others, He has the power to help you. Yet He only helps those who admit their helplessness. He will never abandon or forsake you when you turn to Him. Just as much as offering a gift at the altar is a spiritual exercise, seeking forgiveness and reconciliation is an even more important exercise and an act of obedience (Matthew 5:23-24).

Forgiveness puts the final seal on what happened to hurt you. You will still remember what happened, but you will no longer be enslaved by it. Forgiveness is a wonderful way to honor yourself. It affirms that you deserve to be happy.

Yes, forgiving someone who has hurt you could be the greatest challenge of your life. But there is nothing quite like living in peace, knowing you are a forgiving and forgiven person. May God bless you as you endeavor to seek the truly liberating experience of forgiveness.

UNITE 4 AFRICA

www.Unite4Africa.org

Abducted But Not Forsaken is a story of how God can redeem every experience and every life for His greater purpose. Despite the pain, doubts, and my own weakness, I now look back and clearly see God's expansive, redemptive plan that was unfolding—a plan that now touches tens of thousands of lives with the hope of Christ across Africa and beyond.

Unite 4 Africa is a ministry of community and life transformation throughout the world, including the most unreached and war-torn nations. Over 50 countries have been impacted by meeting the spiritual, physical, medical, social, and emotional needs of people in desperate need.

I give God all the glory for how He has redeemed my story—and I want to invite you to be a part of that unfolding story of hope through Unite 4 Africa, which is supported by the donations of friends who share our passion for demonstrating Christ's love to others.

You can learn more at our website. I would be honored to know that you've chosen to be a part of our support team.

Okongo Samson

Unite 4 Africa, Inc. is a tax-exempt 501(c)(3) organization and is a member of the Evangelical Counsel for Financial Accountability.